# FROM THE INSIDE

"It appears a theology of evangelism falls between a rock and hard place. It either suffers from the silence of systematic theology or when viewed practically it cannot sustain itself in the face of criticism or even be self-critical."

"If leaders are struggling with caring for their own souls, what do we imagine they are modeling to those they lead?"

"Spiritual activity is taking place but it is not making disciples of Jesus Christ. Rather it is producing a "mediocre product.""

"What I would argue … is that the local church is the biblically-ordained and relevant vehicle for transformational discipleship."

"There was a hunger and so young people began to visit our church."

"The real genius of our fellowship is a lay movement."

"Although music was trending among young people the reality of the JPM was not the medium it was the message. 'In other words, while culturally current worship unquestionably attracts people to new paradigm churches, it is equally important to stress that conversion experiences focus on the message and not simply the form of Christianity.'"

"As long as I am alive I'll never let them be diverted."

"Evangelism, [it] is what we are all about. That is done by preaching, but evangelism is what we are called to. To take out of the Gentiles a people for His name. That's what we are called to."

"He was a young twenty-two year old who said to God, 'You can take my life and [if] you can use it in any way for your glory, Lord I'm willing.'"

"It isn't just me who's made disciples, this congregation, this body of believers, they've been involved in the discipleship process as well."

"There [are] some people that know what we do, but when you really grow then you know why we do what we do. And so I wanted to convey the distinctive of those things and the fact that you cannot swerve from that."

"Truth is better caught than taught. The church is a place where people can catch the truth by seeing it for themselves."

"I want them to have what I have and to know that God will work in their lives."

# THE REGIONS BEYOND

## Impacting the World

*From a Small Church in a Small Town*

John W. Gooding

THE REGIONS BEYOND:
"Impacting the World From a Small Church in a Small Town"

Information address:

John W. Gooding, P.O. Box 268, Globe, AZ  85502

*Designed by Larry Beauregard*
*Front Cover photograph by John W. Gooding*

Library of Congress Cataloging-in-Publication Data has been applied for.

ISBN-13: 978-1541040151

**DEDICATION:**

For all the pastors, pioneers and disciples
of the Christian Fellowship worldwide.

# CONTENTS

# PREFACE

I read the original draft of this book that John Gooding wrote for a dissertation. I was gripped by the history of our Fellowship and the fact that John had captured on paper the spirit of what made our Fellowship.

The miracle that God has produced through common people is unique in our generation. We didn't begin with a plan. We just wanted to see people saved. We are the most astounded people of all at what God can do. What is possible with a people who will go back to the Bible and begin to reproduce the pattern of discipleship is astonishing.

A family who recently moved to join with us in Prescott made a profound statement. They said, "We already had joined in the vision for souls; but we found a church that had a vision for the world." That characterized the statement, "Impacting the world from a small church in a small town."

Wayman O. Mitchell
Prescott, November 2016

# ABOUT THE AUTHOR

It seems appropriate to explain the author's interest and involvement in the Christian Fellowship Ministry (CFM). It is more than an academic interest in the CFM story. The author and his wife were born again as young people. Prior to becoming involved in the CFM we had served in a Pentecostal church in Southern California. We felt a call to do more for God. We fasted and prayed for God's direction in early 1976. Because we had some familiarity with the Spanish language and an interest in Mexico, we felt God would lead us to work in orphanages or teaching in Northwestern Mexico. We felt it would be something we could do for God during our summers.

We had a contact with missionaries to Central America and they suggested contacting a Spanish language Bible School. We did and moved to Miracle Valley, Arizona in the fall of 1976. That brought us into contact with the Sierra Vista Foursquare Church. Sierra Vista was a small town in southeastern Arizona. The church had been pioneered six months earlier by a couple from the Prescott Foursquare church and Pastor Wayman Mitchell. The Sierra Vista church was growing rapidly. It was filled with young people. My wife and I were about the same age as the pastor and his wife. That made us the older folks in the congregation. The majority of the congregation was saved out of lifestyles of drug and alcohol addiction. Some were on the verge of divorce but their marriages had been restored. Other couples were "shacking up" and had decided to get married.

Our first Sunday in the church the author's wife was asked to play the piano. She did that morning and for most of the services the next three years. Then on that first Sunday night we witnessed a Jesus People wedding. The couple that had been living together was asked to stand. They were married in the middle of the church service. Then all, bride and groom included, sat down and watched the movie *Thief in the Night*. It's a movie about a newly wed couple and the rapture. One is taken the other is left behind. In the movie the husband is taken in the rapture and the wife is left behind. The music carried the line, "I wish we'd all been ready." An altar call was given and several souls were saved. It wasn't just church doctrine we were seeing. We were seeing transformation. It was revolutionary for us. We had been raised as church kids and accepted Jesus as Lord and Savior when in our teens. We had been taught about the kingdom of God. The church in Sierra Vista made it a reality.

We went to a crusade on Obregon, Mexico over the Thanksgiving holiday and met other pastors from the CFM including Pastor Wayman Mitchell. Then in January of 1977 we attended a conference in Prescott. It was not large and there were only a few pastors and members of their congregations present. But we were moved to such a degree that we told our pastor on Friday night we wanted to be a part of what we saw God was doing. We had not come out of a drug or alcohol lifestyle. We were not hippies. We were not single people. We were married. We were not old but also not as young as the majority of the congregation. We were somewhat of an anomaly in the Fellowship. Nonetheless we welcomed discipleship.

After three years in the Sierra Vista church we felt called to pioneer a church in a small New Mexico town. After a year of non-spectacular ministry we were asked to come on staff in a rapidly growing Colorado church. It was growing at the rate of sixty people every six months. We had never seen anything like it. A year later we were again sent to pastor. We took a church in New Mexico that had suffered through a moral failure. After nearly three years we were called to Arizona and again took over a church that had suffered a moral failure. We saw some success. People were recovered, new people were saved, and we made an attempt to launch a pioneer work. Still feeling stirred for ministry and nearing forty years old we left the pastorate for evangelistic work. First traveling to Australia where we ministered in 24 different churches. These were mostly pioneer churches established out of the Perth, Western Australia CFM church. We were in Australia and New Zealand for five months. Then we went to the United Kingdom, then on to Uganda and Kenya, and then more evangelistic work in the United States. Another time of pastoral work in California followed and then more evangelism.

We felt stirred to missionary work and a door opened in West Africa. We made an attempt to pioneer a church in Liberia. A civil war was brewing and no church was started. Fifty thousand persons starved to death in that war and thousands more fled the country as refugees. Two years later another attempt was made during a time of quasi-peace but it also proved impossible.

Fortunately, over the course of time the Christian Fellowship Church in Sierra Leone has sent workers into Liberia and established a number of churches.

In 1996 we were established in the ministry of the Globe Christian Center. It has been our base of operation and home church since that time. The Globe Christian Center was one of the first pioneer works established out of the Prescott Foursquare Church. It was pioneered in 1976. Globe is a small copper mining town in east-central Arizona. The Globe church has maintained a close relationship with its mother church in Prescott for over forty years. My wife and I have had a relationship with the Prescott Church and its pastor, Wayman Mitchell, since first meeting him on the mission trip to Obregon, Mexico in 1976. These relationships made the dissertation project personally meaningful and important.

Desire to put into the Christian literature this remarkable story was important to the author. What God has accomplished in moving a broken and discouraged church and pastor into a worldwide ministry is important. There are no secret formulas or ideas. The biblical pattern for relationship with Christ and revival has long been established. They are well known to anyone who has cared to look seriously at the issue. Books by Arthur Wallis, Leonard Ravenhill, Oswald Sanders and others published in the early years of the Jesus People Movement and CFM clearly show the issues. The books and writings of other missionaries, pastors and teachers such as David Bosch, Roland Allen, Paul Hiebert and others also point clearly to principles of revival.

The author's primary interest is not academic. It is not historical. This book contains material that is the basis of the Christian Fellowship. There is biblical material. There is relevant material from the Christian literature. There are also insights and discoveries made over the years of Pastor Wayman Mitchell's ministry and life. The author's interest is to tell this remarkable story as an example of the grace and power of God. It is for the people of God. It is for churches that are struggling, broken and/or discouraged. It is for struggling ministers who have no clear direction. It is to provide material that would encourage and stir the common people, the laymen, to pursue the high call of God and see what God would do.

# INTRODUCTION
# TO THE READER

*"How often do we hear about discipline of the Christian
life these days? … I see no hope whatsoever of any true
revival and reawakening until we return to it."*
D. Martyn Lloyd-Jones

This is a story. It is a story of transformation. It is a story of evangelism, discipleship and church planting. It is a story of reaching the nations of the world with the gospel. It is an exciting story. In 1970 the Prescott Foursquare Church in Arizona was struggling. It had been morally violated and broken. It was a small abused congregation. At that time, Prescott was a rural town of about 17,000 persons in northwestern Arizona. Wayman Mitchell took the pastorate in January. The addition of his family increased the size of the congregation to about two-dozen persons. From this small congregation in a small rural community God has raised a movement that has impacted the world. The Christian Fellowship Ministries (CFM), as it is now called, has birthed over twenty-two hundred churches located in one hundred and sixteen nations of the world. This story is meaningful to layman and minister alike. It is important for the broader Christian community. In this story one can see how God can use common men and women and the common things of humanity to minister in the regions beyond.

Writing about the transformation of the Prescott Foursquare Church began with a research project for a dissertation. That was researched and written for an academic community. This book, however, was written for a broader audience. It is intended to be meaningful to laymen and ministers alike. It is intended provide an example of what God can do with people who simply try and follow God. It is intended to inspire persons to the work of God. And it is intended to inspire ministers to the possibilities of God when faced with the impossibilities of the world.

The Bible says Jesus taught them "many things by parables (Mark 4:2)." Jesus used common stories of the world around him to teach spiritual truths. The Prescott Foursquare Church story touches on the common arenas of life. Out of common life comes this powerful example of what God can do. This is not a one-of-a-kind supernatural event. It is the result of simple biblical principles. There was no explosive event that triggered the revival and expansion of the Prescott ministry. It was simple evangelism by local people in a local community.

America in the 1970s was experiencing the Jesus People Movement (JPM). That movement changed America and much of the western world. Principles from that movement became part of the CFM. The language of transformation was common to the Jesus people. When witnessing, Jesus People commonly cited Romans 12:1-2:

> I beseech you therefore, brethren, by the mercies of God, that you present your bodies a living sacrifice, holy, acceptable to God, which is your reasonable service. And do not be conformed to this world, but be transformed by the renewing of your mind, that you may prove what is that good and acceptable and perfect will of God.

The Prescott ministry picked up the importance of transformation for individuals and the church. This part of the story is written in chapter one.

The Great Commission also stirred the Jesus people. There was urgency about winning the world to Jesus The biblical and theological foundation for much of the Christian Fellowship Ministry starts with this commission. The biblical foundation of evangelism, discipleship and church planting is found in Matthew 28:16-20:

> Then the eleven disciples went away into Galilee, to the mountain which Jesus had appointed for them. When they saw Him, they worshiped Him; but some doubted. And Jesus came and spoke to them, saying, "All authority has been given to Me in heaven and on earth. Go therefore and make disciples of all the nations, baptizing them in the name of the Father and of the Son and of the Holy Spirit,

teaching them to observe all things that I have commanded you; and lo, I am with you always, even to the end of the age." Amen.

Chapters two and three establish the biblical and theological grounding of the CFM within the Great commission.

Chapter four is about the discovery of a pattern for the CFM ministry. It is important to note that pattern does not indicate the purpose of this book is a step-by-step guide or methodology for revival. It was out of trial and error, out of a decision here and a decision there, and out of some things that seemed to work that the ministry of the CFM evolved. It was not a discovery of a new doctrine or the implementation of a program that transformed the CFM. It was the discovery of what God was doing and implementing that in the Prescott church. The deeper discovery was that God was restoring the dignity of the local church. The indigenous church principle and the making of disciples propelled the mission forward.

There was a stirring in hearts for the regions beyond the local church. There was a desire to take the gospel to the world. Chapters five and six follow that desire to reach other cultures and nations. These chapters follow God's purposes for the CFM in a loose outline of, a) discovery of a pattern, b) the testing of the pattern and c) finally a pattern that works in the cultures of the world. Chapter five tells of early church planting efforts. The early pattern of church planting was challenged. There was a challenge to continue the early efforts despite setback. Chapter six deals with the continuation of the story to the regions beyond Prescott and the United States.

The concluding chapter (seven) takes up the question of sustainability. The growth and expansion of the CFM depends on many things. Two that are vital are the ministering presence of the Holy Spirit and faithful leadership. Paul admonished Timothy:

> And the things that you have heard from me among many witnesses, commit these to faithful men who will be able to teach others also. (2 Tim. 2:2)

Paul is talking about a sustained ministry through four generations. It is a four-generation span of impartation through discipleship. Faithful men, such as Paul, are to impart their ministry to disciples, such as Timothy, who admonished to impart that spiritual knowledge and example to other faithful men who would also impart it to others. That is discipleship. The Christian world needs to do what Jesus did. Jesus made disciples. Those disciples "turned the world upside down (Acts 17:6)." What must have seemed impossible to a handful of disciples in the first century is no less impossible in the twenty-first. Following chapter seven are notes. These are for those who wish to follow-up various ideas and sources mentioned throughout the text. The research for this book was to find core elements that led a broken church out of brokenness to spiritual health and world impact. This is not a history, formula, or step-by-step guide for revival. It is an example of what God can do with a common people who seek to faithfully obey God.

# 1

# IF TRULY CHRISTIAN

*"All theology is practical, and all practice,*
*if it is truly Christian, is theological."*
Douglas J. Moo

Jesus is risen from the dead!" It is the statement Wayman Mitchell uses to begin his crusade ministry. He continues, "All power in heaven and earth has been given to Him. Jesus has the power to heal you, deliver you and save you." God's promises to bring salvation to the world, to heal the sick and deliver the oppressed are still valid. He adds, "Where two or three are gathered in Jesus name, and there must be two or three here tonight, Jesus is present in power." In these crusades he preaches a biblical message calling for sinners to repent and believe God for salvation and healing. It is a declaration, he explains, and not an explanation. It is a sermon and not a teaching. It is preaching for a response. He asks sinners to respond at the end of the message and then prays for the sick. He prays for a woman who has lupus. He prays for a woman who is deaf and she is healed. He prays for people who are still in pain after being injured in accidents or falls. He prays for women in pain from Caesarian birth of their children.

Wayman Mitchell hasn't always preached and seen miracles in large healing crusades around the world. After experiencing salvation and baptism in the Holy Spirit he went to Bible school and then pastored before coming to Prescott, Arizona in 1970. This book is about a revival or move of God that began then in the Prescott Foursquare Church. It is a move of God that has transcended the barriers of a small, rural church that was broken and discouraged. It is the story of how God, working through a man and men, broke through and became a force in the earth.

It is one story and yet it is many stories as well. It describes what emerged from research that included over fifty interviews, hundreds of sermons, Bible studies, conferences, outreaches and personal relationships covering a nearly fifty-year history. It is the story of what has become the Christian Fellowship Ministries (CFM). It is not just a story. It is an ongoing movement and the final chapters are not yet written. The full impact of the thousands of changed lives has not yet been registered. It is a story of history but also a story of hope. It is a story of hope because what God has done in this story can be repeated in others and in other places. It is a story of the promises of God. Promises, some made four thousand years ago, that are still available for those who will believe them.

The Bible is not an academic research textbook. It contains stories of God's interaction with humankind. Sometimes the Bible is referred to as "His-story." It is more than history. It is God's revelation of himself and his purposes. The Old Testament stories are for our instruction. They are to learn from. In the New Testament there are parables. They are, as someone put it, "stories of intent." In a similar way this story of the Prescott Foursquare Church and its transformation has intent. It is not just for information. Rather, it can become a living reality in any believer who will contend and believe.

There has been a consensus that the Jesus People Movement (JPM) triggered a number of ministries in the late 1960s and early 1970s. The movement of God in Prescott began at that time and it was influential in the formation of the CFM. The ministries that arose out of the hippies and then Jesus People Movement were centered on Christ, the Bible, the Holy Spirit and the hope of Jesus' return. Despite the consensus and the importance of these issues there has been little theological grounding. Perhaps this is due to the anti-intellectual stance and resistance to "doctrine" in the JPM. The Jesus People tended to favor the pragmatic over the intellectual.

The theological parameters held by the JPM have also been foundational for the CFM. Confrontational evangelism and one-on-one witness were primary elements in the JPM. The militant witness of Jesus' power to change lives led to transformation of sinners, transformation of the church culture and transformation of the church vision. Personal witness and evangelism of the lost are not an anomaly of the JPM. They are biblically grounded. The centering scriptures for this include Romans 12:1-2, Matthew 28:16-20, and the Book of Acts. These provide the paradigm of change in believers, the church culture and mission.

Importantly, evangelism did not leave new converts in a vacuum. The real key was involvement in discipleship. The new convert was connected to real ministry. It was a lay ministry and not a professional clergy that pushed the envelope to regions beyond. That led to a focus on church planting and expansion of the CFM to other cities, cultures and nations.

Jesus People of the 70s commonly used the first two verses of Romans twelve to talk about how Jesus could change or transform a person's life. Being born again would change or transform the sinner. They would become a new creation in Jesus (2 Cor. 5:17). Romans 12:2 is an imperative. We are to be transformed. It is not optional. Transformation is the parameter recognized by the Jesus People and the CFM that salvation and a new life has begun.

Romans 12:1-2 comes between a lengthy doctrinal discussion of how a sinner becomes a new person (Chapters 1-11) and a discussion of what being a new person (creation) means in daily life (12:3-15:13). Paul opens this new section of Romans with "Therefore." That is, in the light of what has gone before there is more to say. Paul is perhaps reflecting on the issues of conduct he faced in Corinth or the other churches he has pioneered.[1] His concern in Corinth was to root out a one's own wisdom and self-will and establish one in the perfect will of God.[2] Paul meshes creed (or what is believed) with conduct for an understanding that holiness is neither automatic nor inevitable.[3] The first eleven chapters of Romans do not seem at a casual reading to offer much moral content but the concluding chapters of Romans contain clear exhortations to practice the new life in a real community.

The challenge is to become what the new life explained in chapters one through eleven means in practical life. Instead of a downward spiral of living as a sinner (1:18-32) the readers are to be renewed and live rightly.[4] In chapters 1-11 Paul has established that Jew and Gentile are on equal footing regarding grace and disgrace and concerning salvation and sin.[5] Leon Morris refers to Romans 12:3 and following as "Application." Morris continues, saying, "It is foundational" that the person justified not live as the unjustified sinner rather clearly Paul's theology has a "therefore" regarding human behavior. "All doctrines of justification, grace, election, and final salvation taught in the preceding part of the epistle are made the foundation for the practical duties enjoined in this [part]."[6] Douglas Moo captures the thought with "All theology is practical, and all practice, if it is truly Christian, is theological."[7]

Transformation has important ramifications not only in the individual but also in the community of believers or the church. It speaks of an event and a process that involves the whole person. It is not merely outward adherence to rules and regulations by one's body. It is not merely an inward work of the mind. Transformation means a thing undergoes a change of form or nature— it is literally transformed.[8] Transformation for a church could also go under several common labels such as "revival" or "renewal" churches. Or it could refer to a more modern term such as turn-around or breakout churches.[9]

There is a deeper spiritual nuance that is important. The Old Testament verb *hāpak* "can refer to God's power to transform things from one reality to another."[10] The New Testament term *metamorphoō* is used in the case of Jesus being transfigured on the mountain (Matt. 17:2 and Mark 9:2).[11] In the case of Romans 12:2 *metamorphoō* is used as transformation to a whole new way of thinking. In 2 Corinthians 3:18 it is used to describe change to ever-increasing glory. For Paul in Romans 12:2 transform carries the meaning of an invisible process in a Christian already begun in this present life. It is a process that leads to a new moral life in Christ by the Spirit.

Craig Keener explains in *The Mind of the Spirit: Paul's Approach to Transformed Thinking* that Paul with a beseeching urgency warns believers not to follow the pattern of thinking that is found in unbelievers. This requires a living sacrifice to the reasonableness of the call and will of God. The life of the world is unreasonable. The old mind boasts of knowing God but the renewed mind does the will of God. Its decisions recognize what is good, acceptable and perfect. These are moral criteria for evaluating life. Paul sees behavior as something to be viewed from an eternal perspective and in light of the body of Christ, the church. It is the context of Romans 12:1-2 that establishes the importance of transformation. Verses 3 thru 5 of Romans 12 says,

> For I say, through the grace given to me, to everyone who is
> among you, not to think of himself more highly than he ought

to think, but to think soberly, as God has dealt to each one a measure of faith. (4) For as we have many members in one body, but all the members do not have the same function, (5) so we, being many, are one body in Christ, and individually members of one another. (NKJV)

The scripture continues with the list of gifts set in the body of Christ. The transformation of the mind and the renewal that the Spirit works in the mind is for service in the body. The transformation and renewal are set in the larger context of ministry in the body of Christ. To think "soberly (Rom. 12:3 NKJV)" is to think with a sound or right mind. The transformation of a believer is, therefore, a work that also transforms the culture of the church.[12] Change that is merely outward in form is inadequate for salvation. It is simply becoming more religious.[13]

Ernst Käsemann does not see change as merely a private matter. Change or transformation of an individual has a public and eschatological nature that is important to the world.[14] Transformation or change is essentially the goal of teaching and preaching with the unashamed objective of preserving the true gospel and Word of God. Obedience of individuals to the Word of God is necessary for assimilation of new converts in the church.[15] Transformation and change in a believer's life affects the congregation.

Paul applies the consequences of his messages to daily life[16] reflecting the earlier moral instruction (6:11ff) about living in the present evil era.[17] The transition in Romans to moral instruction in chapters twelve to fifteen is set in the framework of the new eschatological reality. Imperatives dominate these first two verses. Schreiner says "I exhort" should be seen as a command. The two commands to not be conformed and to be transformed should also be seen as imperatives. It is the more difficult reading.[18] Paul alters the Jewish worldview of the New Testament era so that the eschatological age is now present and not just an age to come. The new age is at work in believers currently.[19]

Although Romans 12-15 may appear to be a loosely constructed addition to the theology of chapters 1-11 these verses are not standard paraenesis tacked onto the end of Paul's doctrine. Paul is seeking to establish a relationship with Rome, a community he did not pioneer and does not personally know. He is seeking to establish a community ethos of unity in the midst of diversity (Jew and Gentile).[20] Transformation (verse 2) is part of many religions as a mystery but this is not Paul's thought. Transformation is already operative and reshapes the Jewish hope and the believer's lifestyle. There is certainly an age to come but it is already working within the present age not merely a hope to come and not as a hopeful escape but as part this age.[21] Although easily overlooked, moral instruction is found in the first part of the letter (especially chapters 6 and 8). Romans 12:1-2 expand on the previous parts of Romans and reflect back on the opening chapter's downward spiral of sin.

Readers of Romans are called to present their bodies to God. This language may have roots in a baptismal formula. It is certainly about sacrifice as part of true worship.[22] For Käsemann either the whole of Christian life is worship or else acts such as baptism are absurd.[23] Paul's reaching to the Old Testament idea of sacrifice is important. Paul criticized the Jews for their false reliance on the cult activities of sacrifice. Here Paul draws out the implication that presentation of our bodies is reasonable in the light of the new era of salvation in Jesus.[24] The sacrifice of Jesus does away with animal sacrifices. Paul does not remove sacrifice from faith but extends the concept to the whole person so that every facet of the believer's existence is involved.[25] Being part of a group requires participation in the activities that identify the group. Handing over the body in sacrifice means identification or membership with the group that does the same.[26] The challenge is to belong to the community or the body of Christ. Belonging requires the surrender of one's life to the norms of the whole. This is important because the church is an identifiable entity in this current age. The transformation that occurs in the members also transforms the church. For the broken Prescott Foursquare Church this was essential if it was to move forward. The language of sacrifice and transformation come together in the sense of a community of change.

The new life in Christ is lived by the mercies of God.[27] It comes by the offering of one's person to God. In so doing the person rejects conformity to the world and accepts transformation by the renewal of the mind to accomplish the will of God. The intention of transformation is not simply private but reaches another level empowering the church for transformation of the world. The offering of the body characterizes the change from the old to the new so that God's will becomes the normal conduct of a believer.[28] The command to offer (also 6:13, 16, 19) one's body is in response to the demand to not offer any part of one's mortal body as an instrument of wickedness. Nor can one let sin reign in any part of one's body.[29] Offering spiritual sacrifices is logical worship as in 1 Peter 2:5. "You also, as living stones, are being built up a spiritual house, a holy priesthood, to offer up spiritual sacrifices acceptable to God through Jesus Christ (NKJV)." As the heading in the *New Jerusalem Bible* paraphrases it, "worship worthy of thinking beings".[30]

Offering one's body is a central demand of God. It results from the message of justification and is crucial to one's ability to communicate with the Creator.[31] It means knowing the will or wants of God (Rom 2:18) on a daily or ongoing basis and living accordingly.[32] Offering the body in worship is pleasing to God. Worship expresses itself in concrete acts of service. That is, authentic Christian worship includes the body. It has both negative and positive effects. Sacrifice of the body means either presenting it to God for service or mortifying the body's sinful nature.[33] The presenting of the body in spiritual worship (sacrifice) is not simply the presentation of the fleshly parts but includes the mind as well as the body.

James Dunn says body (*somata*) clearly stands for the whole person in concrete relationship with the world. It is only through the body that one can relate to other persons and only in the concrete realities of daily life.[34] To Witherington change is a "deliberate and stark contrast."[35] Paul is talking about a paradigm change in worldview. "The verbs translated 'conform' and 'transform,' while imperative, are in the present continual sense. Paul is talking about a process of de-enculturation and reorientation."[36] Fitzmyer stresses that in Jesus we are suited for something beyond the cult of animal sacrifice. We are suited by our rational nature to live uprightly before God by offering our whole self for obedience from faith.[37] Käsemann says the decision to offer one's self to God is precisely at the point where it seems irrational. It is irrational in the same vein as the Father sending the Son into the world to save sinners.[38] The Stoic and modern idea of transformation deals with inward transformation. It was not necessarily expressed outwardly.[39] The demand of a bodily sacrifice to God is something designed to shock the Greeks and Jews. It was also shocking to the mystery religions that saw worship as only mystical or inward. And it is shocking today to those who feel religion is only an inward acknowledgement or a belief system.

The meanings of the words conform and transform are debated in scholarly arenas. Witherington comments that outward conformity "seems to be in view here."[40] According to Dunn they are not used to distinguish inward and outward forms.[41] Paul understands social groups, institutions and traditions have the power to mold individual behavior. The imperative tone indicates human responsibility to stop being conformed and instead be transformed. Individuals are responsible to accept or reject these influences and choose the things, actions and thoughts that are in accord with the will of God.[42] This occurs in the process of renewal. It specifically involves the renewing of the mind. Evidence of this concrete change in life is an essential marker of new believers in the CFM as it was in the early JPM.

The terminology of renewal is unique to Christian literature. Renewal of the mind involves the ability to discern or test the will of God. The process is: first the Word of God and the Spirit of God renew the mind, then one is able to discern and desire the will of God and is then increasingly transformed by it. These are the stages of moral transformation of the believer.[43] Renewal is necessary for Jew and Gentile. If Paul were asked about the source of renewal, Dunn says Paul would respond saying, "The Spirit."[44] This is supported by 2 Corinthians 3:18, "But we all … are being transformed into the same image from glory to glory, just as by the Spirit of the Lord (NKJV)." And Paul writes to Titus, "According to His mercy He saved us, through the washing of regeneration and renewing of the Holy Spirit (3:5 NKJV)." Moo describes renewal as a process that is internal. "The fact that calls on believers to engage in this renewing of the mind shows that it does not automatically happen to us when we believe."[45] It is an internal process that produces fruit pleasing to God.[46]

There are still commands that impinge in an obligatory way on believers. The expectation of renewal is not for mere obedience but rather moral discernment.[47] It is a rationality that is fitting and distinguishes humankind from the rest of creation. Humans are not beasts. The renewed mind is one of critical judgment by Christians that can differentiate and accept what is fitting. Ultimately the purpose of the sacrificed body and the renewed mind are not for the fulfillment of self's desires but to serve and think in terms of the greater body of Christ.[48] Only God's will is fitting and it involves but is not restricted to the moral arena.[49]

Dunn points to the ability to form the correct ethical judgment and then comments that Paul is "probably thinking of a corporate and not merely individual process." He points out that the remaining elements of Romans form the foundation of Christian ethics. Paul's intention in Romans is not an uncritical comment on common household codes of justice and behavior but to establish a theological grounding. It is a more fundamental intention. Paul intends that the church in Rome be a transforming influence in society. Because a person has a concrete relationship with the world and with the church there can be a corporate force for change in the world.[50] It is at this point Paul co-opts the cultural convention to empower the church for transformation of society.[51] Worship is the way we live and not just what we do on Sunday morning.[52] "True worship means agreement with God's will to his praise in thought, will, and act."[53] It is completely reasonable for believers to radically dedicate themselves wholly to God.[54] This is exactly what the world says is unreasonable. This is the challenge for every beleaguered church. There must be renewal individually and therefore corporately.

There are only two models for believers to mold their values to—the value system of the world and the value system of God. "These two value systems (*this world* and *God's will*) are incompatible, even in direct collision with one another," according to John Stott. He continues saying, "The two sets of standards diverge so completely that there is no possibility of compromise."[55] This present evil age cannot be the regulative principle. Conformity to this age results in an unfit mind. Radical renewal is possible because the new age has begun and is advanced by every decision and ends in the glory of God.[56] Renewal is a day-by-day progress (2 Cor. 4:16, Col 3:10). "The Christian finds out the will of God not to contemplate it but to do it. It goes without saying that what is known to be God's will is—perfect."[57]

The Prescott Foursquare Church needed renewal. The inward brokenness of a violated people and the outward discouragement had to first be transformed. This is akin to the efforts needed by Hezekiah and Josiah for renewal in the nation. Jesus People have been described as "restorationists" or "primitivists," that is, they seek a renewal of the old paths. This is what was sought in Prescott.

Jesus came into the world to save sinners or, to put it differently, to save the world. That means change. Change is both necessary and painful for a church that has been traumatized. When Wayman Mitchell accepted the pastorate of the Prescott Foursquare Church he understood change was necessary. The JPM was peaking in popularity and influence. It was centered on Christ, the Bible, conversions, the Holy Spirit, and the end times. Mitchell adapted the JPM strategies and principles to his own view of God's call to bring about a transformation of the church and its ministry.

The theological foundation for grounding transformation was found in Romans 12:1-2 and Matthew 28:16-20. Romans 12 provided the theological framework for the "new life" of believers leading as it does to the practical aspects of what kind of life a new believer is to live. The command to be transformed to a Christian lifestyle by renewal of the mind and the sacrifice of the body for service in the church were important elements incorporated in the CFM. Transformation of the lives of new converts and the older core of believers resulted in a new vision and hope in the congregation.

That new vision and hope moved them to see the Great Commission of Matthew 28 as their own mission. The scope of Matthew 28 encompassed the call to witness to the lost and to become followers of Jesus through a radical commitment and costly discipleship. Disciples sent into the world as evangelists brought about the church planting they saw in the book of Acts.

The theological grounding does not rest upon only a few scriptures. Transformation is found as a theme throughout Romans. It is echoed in 1:24, 25, 28; 2:18; and 6:13, 16, 19. The sacrifice of the body is echoed in Romans 6:6; 7:4, 24; 8:10, 11, 13, 23 and renewal of the mind in 7:23, 25.[58] Change and new life are found throughout the scriptures in the numerous miracles such as the deliverance of the demoniac in Gadara and the transformation of the lives of the disciples as well.

The scope of the Great Commission in Matthew 28 is broad indeed. Making disciples implies that in going there is proclamation or evangelism calling for a decision about the reign of God. It implies witness and is connected to the Commission by Jesus in Acts 1:8. Calling is implied. Moses was called (Exod. 3:1-4, 16), Gideon was called (Judg. 6:11-21), Jeremiah was called (Jer. 1:1-4) and other examples show clearly there is calling for service in the kingdom of God.[59] Likewise, the disciples were called and hence the application today for followers of Jesus.

Jesus connects the Commission to the coming and empowering of the Holy Spirit in Acts 1:8 and Luke 24:47-49. Preaching repentance and forgiveness to all nations before the end of the age is empowered by the Holy Spirit. The Second Coming implied in the Great Commission gives an urgency and priority to making disciples. Evangelism, witness, discipleship, new life, sending and church planting of the CFM flow out of an understanding of transformation. Transformation of the life and mindset is necessary to pursue the Great Commission. It is not to be assumed that this is the sum of all that occurs in and through the CFM. It cannot be assumed that many other viable and necessary ministries of the CFM are invalid or ignored. Conversion to a new life and commitment to The Great Commission began the work of renewing a broken and disillusioned church for service to their Lord and Savior. It all began very simply. As F. F. Bruce says, "Those who believed the good news carried it to others."[60]

# 2
# THE FORTY WORDS

*"It is impossible to say anything greater and
more than this in only forty words."*
Adolf Harnack

Admittedly little has been done with the theological and biblical grounding of the JPM and even less concerning the CFM. There is, however, a large consensus that Christ, the Bible, and evangelism based on the expectation of Jesus' Second Coming are firmly part of the JPM and CFM. The JPM was centered on the Great Commission of Matthew 28:16-20.

It is important to look more closely at this passage in Matthew. David Di Sabatino says the JPM was pneumacentric, Christocentric and apocalyptic.[1] The expectation is to look for these themes in this popularly referenced scripture. One can make the case that within these verses or the "forty words" of the Great Commission the themes of evangelism, witness, discipleship, sending, church planting, empowerment of the Holy Spirit, and the age to come can be found.

After the resurrection the eleven disciples traveled to a prearranged mountain in Galilee to meet Jesus. Some traditions say it was Mount Tabor, the traditional site of the transfiguration, and others say it was the site of the Sermon on the Mount where Jesus could refresh their memories with the words "everything I have commanded you."[2] Others say it was only a place recognized by the disciples and Jesus. Mountains figure prominently in Matthew (16 times) as sites of revelation or perhaps the theme of a new Sinai.[3] Coming as it does at the end of Matthew these words suggest more than just another narrative. This is the last of six discourses of Matthew that Michael J. Wilkins says lead to highlighting the importance of this text.[4] It is a summary of the aim and purpose of Matthew's gospel.

David J. Bosch says New Testament scholarship for many years paid little attention to this passage and perhaps even thought it was a later addition. Eventually in the early part of the twentieth century scholars took note. Bosch translates from Adolf Harnack, "It is impossible to say anything greater and more than this in only forty words."[5] It was Matthew's missionary vision that moved him to write his gospel. He did not set out to write a "Life of Jesus" but to guide the early church through crises by giving it an understanding of its calling and mission. Matthew is essentially a missionary text[6] and the parallel texts in Luke 24:47 and John 20:21 (and Mark 16:15)[7] reflect perhaps differing traditions but similar thought. The multiple attestation of mission suggests the accuracy of Jesus commission. It was not, however, until the 1940s that scholars began to pay serious attention to these forty words and their pivotal nature.

Today scholars agree that the entire gospel of Matthew points to these pivotal words, calling them the "theological program of Matthew," "the climax of the gospel," "a manifesto," and Matthew's "the table of contents".[8] Agreed upon almost universally is that these words cannot be lifted from the rest of Matthew's text without their becoming a mere slogan. It is perhaps the most Matthean part of Matthew. Virtually every word in the text is peculiar to Matthew and this first gospel.[9] It is recognized as unique to Matthew by most.[10] Hagner says, "These words … distill the outlook and various emphases of the Gospel."[11] France notes that it is theologically possible to read from these final words back into earlier chapters to illuminate their significance.[12]

The combination of authority and mission in this passage ("all power" and "make disciples") is also found in Luke 24:47 (his "name" and "all nations") and John 20:21 (the "authority" of the Father and I am sending you). The arrangement of final instructions in Matthew and the parallel accounts of Luke and John announce the fulfillment of the limited mission of Matthew 10:1-5 where Jesus sent the disciples to the lost sheep of the House of Israel. Jesus expands the mission to the Gentiles but does not replace the mission to Israel. The result of the expanded mission is the establishment of the new community (*ekklesia*) fulfilling Jesus' words of Matthew 16:18, "I will build My church and the gates of Hades shall not prevail against it (NKJV)."[13]

The Commission comes together in the fearless and authoritative preaching of the risen Jesus. The mission to preach to the ends of the earth, thus establishing the new community (the church) of the kingdom. The church now in existence started from a handful of doubting, confused and powerless disciples responding to these words given on an unknown hillside (mountain) in Galilee. They waited for the empowering of the Holy Spirit and then starting in Jerusalem pursued the call to go to all nations and make disciples.

The Great Commission contains one primary or central command, the imperative "make disciples," with three subordinate ones (participles); "going," "baptizing" and "teaching." There have been two views on this form, one with a strong emphasis on "go" and the other on "make disciples." Cleon Rogers claims the imperative or commandment idea to "make disciples" is to be preferred because the connotation is set by the verb *mathēteuō* (make disciples).[14] Robert Coleman says *mathēteuō* is the "true verb" in the passage and is the source of emphasis for the word "go."[15] Similar constructions are found in Matthew 17:27 ("go to the sea, cast in a hook) where Peter is given a specific task and in Matthew 28:7 when women are given a task (go quickly and tell His disciples) to report that Jesus is risen from the dead.[16] The purpose of the command to go is to make disciples. The imperative command gives the thrust of the mission and the three participles describe the various aspects of mission with the force of the imperative command,[17] "which is to say, one command that is carried out three ways."[18] The participle "going" could be read as "on your way," "as you go" or "having gone."[19] A parallel is found in the mission of the twelve where Jesus says in Matthew 10:7 "as you go preach (NIV)." The word "make disciples" is to be understood in a rabbinic sense or Jewish context of a student in relationship to a highly esteemed master.[20] The passage has a two-fold relationship in the conclusion of Matthew tying together the resurrection narrative and the most notable points of Matthew's teaching—Christology, discipleship, ecclesiology and future hope.[21]

That Matthew 28 is a commission or even The Great Commission is not universally ascribed to this passage. Francis Beare claims the entire passage and the parallels of Jesus' sending of the twelve in Mark 6:7-11, Matthew 10:1-10 and Luke 9:1-6 are contrasts Matthew uses set against chapter 28 to teach about discipleship.[22] It is true that teaching about discipleship is found in these scriptures but it seems unlikely that Matthew uses them only in that sense. Imbedded in discipleship is the mission to the world that seems to be the theme of Matthew's gospel.

Grant R. Osborne points out there are some who do not see a mission or summary statement in Matthew's ending. Some see an epiphany or exaltation story because of Jesus' new status as the Son of Man following his resurrection. The idea of exaltation parallels that of Ephesians 1:21 in Philippians ("far above all rule and authority," and exalted, highest place, name above all names, 2:9ff) and Colossians ("over all creation," 1:15). Others see it as a royal enthronement similar to the Old Testament passage "I will make the nations your inheritance, the ends of the earth your possession (Ps 2:8)."[23] These parallels reflect an important aspect of the exalted Jesus. It does not seem that this is the main idea of the Great Commission. For Keener "going remains an essential part of the commission."[24] Matthew's statement and context of the Great Commission reflect the reason and meaning of Jesus' resurrection.

"The Great Commission is not an idea tacked inelegantly to the end of Matthew's Gospel, as if Matthew had nowhere else to put it. Rather, it summarizes the heart of this Gospel's message."[25] Osborne adds, "Matthew did not simply repeat that command. He lived it—and so must we. For Matthew, it summed up his entire theology. We must ask whether it summarizes ours."[26] It was in many ways a summary of the JPM and provides a centering focus for the CFM. "Jesus, risen from the dead," becomes the proclamation to the world for the expansion of the kingdom of God and the church.

Matthew connects the command of making disciples with the words "of all nations." For the Jews this was a striking new development.[27] Jesus, on the basis of his authority commissions the disciples to make disciples "having gone" to all nations.[28] Craig S. Keener says, "Ancient hearers would and modern hearers should recognize a drastic innovation in the command to disciple all nations."[29] Wilkins says the theme of God's salvation being universally available climaxes the whole book of Matthew.[30] This universal availability of salvation is hinted at in Matthew 1:1, 2:1-12, 8:5-13 and 15:21-28. The fulfillment of the task of the New Testament church is through witness (Acts 1:8) to the ends of the earth and proclamation (Col. 1:23) to every creature under heaven.[31] The all (*pas*; all authority, all nations, all things) signals the inclusive nature of salvation with the most difficult or troublesome issue for the disciples being the commission to Samaria.[32] The mission to the nations is extremely important if a church is to reach or have a multicultural dimension. Most people groups are parochial and an intentional strategy to incorporate non-members is generally met with strong opposition.

There has been some contention over what "all nations" means. Certainly the Jesus People and the CFM have understood it to mean simply every nation or all peoples on the earth. But Douglas R. A. Hare and Daniel J. Harrington say the phrase *panta ta ethnē* is not transparently clear. They ask if the phrase includes the nation of Israel or is there a deliberate contrast between Jews and Gentiles? Their contention is that in Matthew 21:43 God has taken the kingdom from Israel and given it to the church. The time of Jewish mission was Matthew 10:5. Although Jews may still be incorporated into the church Israel has been replaced by the church.[33] Nolland notes the similar phrase in 24:14 where the gospel of the kingdom will be preached as a testimony "to all nations" (*pasin tois ethnēsin*).[34] The phrase is also found in Matthew 24:9 and 25:32. It occurs where all the nations are gathered together for judgment. The scope of the mission is generally agreed to be a universal mission without discrimination between the Gentile and Jew. Matthew does not suggest that God has given up on the Jews.[35] Wilkins agrees saying most scholars agree that it means all nations inclusive of Israel as the natural meaning of the terms.[36] Some believe a better translation would be "all people groups."[37] It seems most natural to include the Jews in the scheme of the Great Commission as certainly the New Testament church did. The disciples and Paul went first to the synagogues to preach the good news. And in Ephesians Paul makes the point of Jesus mission the making of the two (Jew and Gentile), one body.

The commission Jesus gave in his parting words recorded by all four gospel writers had practical meaning for the disciples. "Going" seems to imply a number of things including witness (Acts 1:8), evangelism, discipleship, sending and church planting.

The task of presenting in this limited space a theology of evangelism is made difficult for two reasons. First it has been given limited attention. It is almost a foregone conclusion and has been left dangling in systematic theology. Only a few words about it are attached to the theology of the church. Wayne Grudem expresses it as a task or purpose of the church from Luke 6:35-36. The church is to worship (ministry to God), nurture (ministry to believers) and evangelize with mercy (ministry to the world by loving enemies and doing good).[38] Duffield and Van Cleave say evangelism is the primary mission of the church given by Jesus before his ascension.[39] However they go on in the next three pages to list evangelism as one of eight purposes of the church and evangelism is in fifth place. They add Romans 15:19-21, "from Jerusalem and round about to Illyricum I have fully preached the gospel of Christ (NKJV)," as its only biblical basis.[40] Millard Erickson places evangelism in the purpose of the church as Jesus' command saying obedience shows a love for Christ.[41] It appears a theology of evangelism falls between a rock and hard place. It either suffers from the silence of systematic theology or when viewed practically it cannot sustain itself in the face of criticism or even be self-critical.[42] The theology of evangelism suffers from shortsightedness by not connecting it with the overall task of the Great Commission in a meaningful way.

A wise man said, "Any religion that does not consider itself valuable enough to share with nonbelievers is fated to crumble from within." Who said it? Not Billy Graham, not any famous Evangelist we've heard of, in fact, it was not even a Christian. It was Yosef Abramowitz, in an article to fellow Jews, taking on the Southern Baptist. He made the comment following the Southern Baptist Convention of 1999 where they voted to dedicate an entire year to evangelizing Jews. He said, "If Jews shrink from the task of proselytizing, it might send a signal that Judaism isn't worth spreading to others."[43] Indeed, the same could be said if Christians fail to evangelize.

Richard Mouw, the former President of Fuller Seminary, reports that at one of his talks he was asked about what books he would still like to write. He replied that he was thinking about what he now sees as mistakes he has made. His wife, in audience, said in a loud voice, "And that will have to be a very long book!" It got a big laugh.

"One such mistake," he said, "has to do with evangelism."

"Back in the 1970's when I and other Evangelical social activists were making the case for what I called 'political evangelism,' I regularly complained about what I saw as too strong an emphasis among Evangelicals on personal evangelism, at the expense of such things as addressing the physical needs of the poor and working in the political arena. One of the choruses from my youth that I often cited as an example of a fundamentalist distortion of the Christian life had this refrain: 'Saved, saved to tell others.' We aren't simply saved to tell others, I would insist. We are saved to participate in a community that shows forth the will of God for all dimensions of human life."

Mouw concluded, "I worry about the unintended effects of that way of putting it."[44]

A noted mega-church and early 'seeker church' pastor has noticed a common mistake in setting the mission statement of a church. Commonly church priorities are set in such a way that evangelism is given a kind of equal standing with other important goals. We have a special tendency to downplay evangelism," so that when it is assigned a place of equal value with other areas of Christian mission, it actually ends up down the scale of priorities."

"Only when we emphasize evangelism above all else will it receive its due." We cannot simply put evangelism on a longer 'to do' list and hope that the Christian community (believers) will carry it out with the appropriate passion.

The proclamation of the gospel is often seen as an end in itself. Proclamation either alone or proclamation with a decision are seen as a completed process. William Abraham points out the problem. Thinking of proclamation alone disconnects the local church from its life as the body of Christ. It creates an attitude that any entrepreneur with no connection to the local church can engage in this crucial ministry. And the other part of the problem is that proclamation alone cannot create a sense of personal ownership of the gospel that can be embraced by the hearer.[45] The Great Commission, however, does not imply that proclamation is the end of the task. It does not imply that church growth is the end of the task. Yet both of these viewpoints are common and both circumvent the true issue of the Great Commission—making disciples.

In his two-volume history and analysis of the early church mission, Eckhard Schnabel says that, with possible and limited exception of the Jews, no religious community made such exclusive claims concerning salvation as the Christian community. No religious community gave such a central place to a historical person as the Christian community. No religious community engaged in deliberate missionary expansion with such clear and strategic goals with a result-oriented implementation as the first Christians.[46] Ferdinand Hahn said:

> The early church was a missionary church. The proclamation, the teaching, all activities of the early Christians had a missionary dimension. The fact that it is not possible to find a defined concept of 'missions' in the New Testament does not alter the fact that early Christianity was controlled by the missionary task in their entire existence and in all their activities.[47]

Schnabel says that Hahn is certainly correct and, "No scholar doubts that the first Christians actively spread their faith, doing missionary work."[48] What is important to understand in the light of the commission to make disciples is that Christian mission is not a matter of getting a confession of faith or establishing a morality but producing disciples. The commission is not found in the means of proclamation but on the product—disciples."[49] The product of the church is a disciple. Marketing does not establish moral criteria or truth and what the church calls mission is not just about proclamation or evangelism. It is about making disciples for the multiplying of the work by adding committed laborers.[50] It is not enough to hear the message of Jesus. There must be a response with the same whole hearted commitment required of those who became disciples of Jesus.[51]

The content of the proclamation of the Word of God is rich and deep. It is "fundamentally simple it is not simplistic; while affirmative, it is never trivial or cheap."[52] The Prescott CFM and other CFM churches have been from the beginning militant evangelists. Mitchell recognized that the secret to keeping and nurturing new converts was in pointing them to a purpose. He pointed them to Matthew 28 and the task of world evangelism.[53] In a sermon, Greg Mitchell said, "It became clear … that our call [as a fellowship] is to take the gospel beyond the four walls of the church, rather than sitting in the church building and hoping that sinners somehow will come."[54] Evangelism is presented in the CFM churches as a call to every believer. It is often referenced as an implication of the Great Commission. The song "Go Ye" was a standard choir presentation on the final night of the international conferences in the

1970s and early 1980s. It set the tone for the announcements of new churches that followed the concluding sermon of the conferences.

Church growth has been an issue for a number of decades. Interest was stirred by the publication of *Bridges of God* by Donald McGavran in 1955.[55] McGavran was the impetus for what has been called the Church Growth School of Missiology. His ideas developed out of his experiences as a missionary in India. In India he noticed what all can see—some churches grow and others stagnate. He attributed the difference to methodology. McGavran saw the primary methodology of establishing a mission station as a contradiction. Mission implied going and station implied staying. What McGavran saw was converts removed from their local setting and placed at the mission station detaching them from their community and the local church. The impact was twofold. First, being transplanted to an essentially alien culture meant they could no longer influence their non-Christian friends, relatives and neighbors. Meanwhile they learned an ethic and language foreign to their culture. The other effect McGavran saw was that resources to sustain the station and the families of the new converts were spent outside of the communities the mission said they were trying to reach. The overall impact was that local church growth stopped or stagnated.

Lesslie Newbigin was also a missionary to India and summarized these effects in *The Open Secret*.[56] Newbigin does not dispute McGavran's view of the facts. "McGavran is right to press the question, 'Why is there not more concern for the multiplication of believers and more evidence of its happening?'"[57] Newbigin says, "Anyone who knows Jesus Christ as Lord and Savior must desire ardently that others should share that knowledge and must rejoice when the number who do is multiplied."[58] Certainly the New Testament records increasing numbers in the kingdom. There were 3000 on the day of Pentecost, then another 5000 in Acts 5, and multiplication of disciples and churches in Acts 6, and increase of the Word in Acts 12. It is right, adds Newbigin, believers should question why their church does not grow and why churches and believers are not concerned about the multitudes that have either not heard the gospel or have rejected it.[59] Why is there not the seemingly spontaneous growth of the church as we see in the ministry of Paul and the New Testament?[60] McGavran rightly raised these questions and it seems the answer must certainly be found in discipleship.

The task of taking the gospel to the whole world was monumental in Jesus day. The burgeoning population of the world today and the unsurpassed growth of technology tempt one to look for other methods of fulfilling the Great Commission. However, as Keener says, "This commission was no afterthought … It summarizes much of the heart of [Matthew's] message."[61] It is a fitting conclusion brought to bear on the reader by the Holy Spirit. There is, according to Graham Duncan, a clear link between the command to make disciples in Matthew 28 and the command in Romans 12 to be transformed.[62] Transformation and the disciplines demanded by discipleship are linked. Discipline releases rather than hampers true growth.

The costs of discipleship are not hidden in the Scriptures. Ralph Martin looking at Acts 14:22 says, "Discipleship is a costly commitment, and there is no easy road to glory."[63] It is a choice that does not allow excuses or postponement. He says that although there is promise of exaltation Jesus demand has been "intensified and deepened" by Luke's addition of hating family relations (Luke 14:26). Most of all, he has added, "even his own life also" as part of the total demand."[64] It is a choice to finish regardless of the costs. It is a choice to establish a priority over family, surrender control of wealth and take up a cross of self-denial.

Craig Keener sees the demand for a cross—a symbol of execution—as the greatest demand in discipleship.[65] It means a priority of Jesus over job security (Matt. 4:19-20), over residential security (Matt. 8:18-20), over financial security (Matt. 19:21) and over cultural obligations (Matt. 8:21-22). It means a cost in marriage and family (Peter was already married). It means having no permanent place (Jesus with no place to lay his head). It means sacrificing financial gain (the rich young ruler's reluctance). It means going against a myriad of social norms (let the dead bury the dead).[66]

Discipleship is not a popular cultural calling. It has a destiny linked to it. Jesus confronted people and demanded a decision for or against God's rule.[67] "Those who would be his disciples must prepare the way for [Jesus'] future coming as John the Baptist did for his first (3:1-3)."[68]

John was arrested, unjustly treated and killed without trial. The disciple can expect to be unjustly judged, misunderstood and maligned. All of the demands of discipleship come with the promise that Jesus will be with his disciples during times of wars and famines (24:6-8) until the kingdom is proclaimed among all peoples (24:14) and until the end.[69] It was into the world that the disciples were sent. They were a somewhat odd group that Jesus commissioned to carry the good news to the world. Willimon writes, "How odd of God," to choose these disciples and us to be preachers.

The Gospel of John and John's epistles emphasize that Jesus was sent (John 3:17, 6:33, 51, 1 John 4:9, 14) to the world that it might be saved.[70] As is common in John's gospel the term "world" is representative of humanity that is hostile to God. Yet it is from that same hostile humanity that Jesus saves and sends individuals with his gospel of salvation.[71] The sending of the disciples into the world is after the manner of the Father sending Jesus (John 17:18, 20:21). "Not all believers in the community [of faith] have the same role as the first disciples, but the community as a whole shares the same mission and purpose: to make Christ known."[72] This makes Jesus the model of what it means to be sent.[73]

Luke's gospel records the sending of the larger group of disciples suggesting that the evangelistic mission was not limited to the apostles or an official commissioning action. "Rather, [Luke] presents an account of a Spirit-inspired spontaneous mission which includes apostles, the seventy, and other unnamed witnesses."[74] Paul, as Mark Keown views Luke-Acts, functioned in a mission mode that stimulated his converts to evangelize. They took the gospel they had received to their family networks (Lydia, the Philippian jailor and on Malta) and throughout their regions of influence (the city of Ephesus, the Lycus Valley).[75]

Paul's proactive strategy for evangelism reached from Antioch to Ephesus and beyond. The most obvious statement of what Paul's church planting mission accomplished is in 1 Thessalonians 1:6-8, "You became imitators of us and of the Lord, for you welcomed the message in the midst of severe suffering with the joy given by the Holy Spirit. And so you became a model to all the believers in Macedonia and Achaia (NIV)."

Paul saw himself as "sent" (1 Cor. 1:17) to preach making it his aim to preach where Christ was not known (Rom. 15:20).[76] His letter to the Colossian believers reveals his understanding that he has been assigned by God to bring about maturity in believers even in churches he did not pioneer or visit such as Colossae. Paul felt a personal responsibility to see that Epaphras' ministry didn't fail because of the heresy that threatened the church.[77] Paul told the Romans that his interest in coming to them was his calling as an apostle that included a mission of bringing people to an obedience of the faith (1:5-6, 15:16-17).[78] Paul's preaching on Mars Hill was part of what Paul saw as a mission to the world. It was consistent with his application of the biblical principle of evangelizing people who have not heard the good news.[79] Paul preached for results. He desired that his hearers be saved, become obedient to the faith, and heed the commandments and call of Christ.[80] It had impact in his generation. It must have impact in our generation. Keener notes that in 1830 there were one billion people in the world. In 1930 there were two billion persons on the earth. Today humanity numbers over seven billion souls. He invites believers to devote all to mobilize the church to fulfill Christ's mission and says that God's power will be commensurate to the task.[81]

Luke adds to his gospel of Jesus (Luke) the Book of Acts. Luke is a historian in the ancient mold and in Acts he explores the roots of the new Christian community. Darrell Bock says:

> Acts is a piece of Hellenistic and Jewish historiography that treats the theme of how the new community [the church] is rooted in God's old promises, the Lord Jesus's current activity, and the Spirit's effective presence. Acts focuses on key human players as well, such as Peter, Stephen, Philip, Paul and James. The book places these characters and events in the contexts of the world's larger history.[82]

Bock sees Acts as answering important questions about God and the gospel: How can salvation come from God and the Jews and also include gentiles? How is salvation the promise of God and yet the Jews reject it? What role does Jesus have? What does the faithful witness accomplish? In spite of these questions Luke raises he says the real center of Acts is God.[83]

Eckhard Schnabel finds the story of the church in Acts. He says the story of the church in Jerusalem covers chapters 1-7. The story of the church in Samaria, Damascus, Caesarea, and Antioch is found in chapters 8-12.

The story of the church in Asia Minor and into Europe is told in chapters 13-20. The book concludes with the impact of the church reaching to Rome resulting in the trial of Paul in chapters 21-28.[84] Schnabel claims the mission of the church is obedience to the divine commission and it is no coincidence that the identity of the church as God's people and the mission as witness is the theme of the first section of narrative in Acts.[85]

In Acts 1:8 Jesus fulfills the divine function of establishing his own witnesses (Isa. 43:10, 12; 44:8-9) and lays out their mission (Isa. 49:6). Jesus uses witness in the legal sense of someone who helps establish the facts. A witness declares the facts. The disciples direct and real experience of Jesus' death and resurrection qualifies them as witnesses. The Old Testament provides a precedent for witnesses. Numbers 35:30 (Deut. 17:6-7) establish the need for multiple witnesses in capital cases. Jesus calls the disciples to receive the enabling of the Holy Spirit and be witnesses of him to the ends of the earth. Witness is not the explanation of times and seasons, or the time of the end. The witness is of the Life, death and resurrection of Jesus. In Acts the witness of Jesus results in the spread of the Word of God, the multiplication of disciples and the establishing of churches.

The biblical case for church planting is more modest than many assume. Arguably there is no need for a biblical foundation of church planting just as there is no need of one for many of the things churches do—revival services, evangelism, secretaries, bookkeepers and a myriad of other things. There are plenty of good reasons for church planting.[86] However, two things need to be kept separated. The biblical rationale for church planting is not the same thing as the biblical guidelines of how to plant a church. Church planting is based on the Great Commission, the central place of the church in the purposes of God and the methodology of the first century work of the apostles.[87] Hence the Book of Acts is probably the most relevant portion of the New Testament for establishing a rationale for church planting. Acts 14:21-28 recounts Paul's activities in Derbe, Iconium and Lystra and the return to Antioch reporting back to the church that sent him out on the mission. It is a good summary statement of the activities involved in planting churches.

Church planting is what happened as a result of obedience to the Great Commission. It is not generally a part of systematic theologies. It has even less a place than evangelism. It can be legitimately subsumed under either missiology or ecclesiology.[88] Historically mission was used to define the acts of God under the heading of *missio dei*.[89] There are three components of a theology of church planting listed by Stuart Murray in his *Church Planting: Laying the Foundations*. Church planting involves the *missio dei* (the mission of God), the incarnation and the kingdom of God.[90] The *missio dei* cannot be reduced to evangelism, discipleship or church planting.[91] It is part of the kingdom of God. The church is a place where kingdom activity takes place. Church planting is larger than evangelism and larger than discipleship. Nonetheless it cannot function apart from evangelism and discipleship. Stuart Murray agrees with Bosch (*Witness to the World*) that "for Protestants as others, mission came primarily to mean the planting of churches. This development was an important deviation from the pietistic view of mission as being first and foremost concerned with the saving of individual souls."[92] Murray and Paul Bowers see Paul's mission as bringing into being Christian communities [churches]. Conversion meant incorporation into a community.[93]

The evangelistic endeavor for Paul was larger than evangelism. "For him it was a mission that embraced evangelism within an ecclesiastical intention."[94] His mission was devoted to the emergence of church communities but went beyond just starting churches. Paul revisited and wrote letters to them. He revisited to strengthen them (Acts 15:36, 16:1-5) and to nurture them as a father (1 Thess. 2:10-12). Paul's letters also indicate his desire for their success and continuing growth in the faith.[95] Paul writes of his great desire to see the Thessalonians (1 Thess. 2:17-18; 3:1-5, 10-11) and reports of finishing or fulfilling his role in one region before moving on to another un-evangelized region.[96] To the Philippians Paul claims he is torn with a desire to depart and be with the Lord and a desire to remain with them for their sake (Phil. 1:24-27). We gather from Paul's ministry that he was committed to founding churches that continued to thrive and have impact even multiplying disciples and leaders as in Ephesus (Acts 20:17).

Paul's ministry and Acts are not the sole indicators of a rationale for church planting. Murray says,

The New Testament can and should be read as a mission document … Every strand of the New Testament teaching, it seems, can be mined for perspectives on church planting. This breadth of material clarifies why it is difficult to find a succinct biblical rationale for church planting.[97]

The simple "proclaiming the gospel" that Paul uses to describe his missionary activity belies the scope of his activities. Beginning with evangelistic preaching, Paul moved on to contending for a response and founding Christian communities that remained firm. Paul's missionary vocation finds fulfillment in well established churches.[98] These churches were not all that was established. From a handful of churches in Paul's day to hundreds within a century of Christ's resurrection tells an even greater story. Stuart Murray says, "Self-propagation or reproduction is not just an admirable quality of some churches, but integral to the definition of the church."[99]

# 3
# A DISTINCTIVE PEOPLE

*"The apocalyptic is the mother of all theology."*
Ernst Käsemann

The theological and cultural identity of the CFM is rooted in the Jesus People Movement. Although the Jesus People Movement peaked in influence in the early 1970s there are at least eight ministries that remain viable today. Calvary Chapel Ministries remain a strong group, usually having one or more of their churches in the top twenty largest churches in the United States. They are centered on the biblical teaching of Chuck Smith (1927-2013). The Vineyard Christian Fellowship remains strong in church planting and music ministries based on the teachings of John Wimber (1934-1997). The Gospel Outreach emphasized praxis of the Word but only a small remnant remains. Jesus People USA is well known but anchored today on their magazine *Cornerstone* and their *Cornerstone Festival*. Maranatha Campus Ministries and Dove Christian Fellowship International are small but viable ministries. Hope Chapel and her daughter churches are still affiliated with the International Church of the Foursquare Gospel but are functionally independent. The Potter's House Foursquare Church and the resulting Christian Fellowship Ministries (CFM), or the Potter's House Christian Fellowship (PHCF), are now an international movement.[1]

The identity of the JPM provides a baseline for understanding these continuing elements and the CFM. David Di Sabatino's exhaustive bibliography of the movement led him to also describe the Jesus People Movement's spiritual theme as primitivistic, and pneumacentric.[2] Beliefs of the JPM concerning Jesus include the virgin birth, death of Jesus as atonement for humanity's sins, bodily resurrection, and physical return to earth to establish the kingdom of God.[3]

Jesus People were experimentalists spiritually but had a penchant for a literal reading of the Bible. They felt they were the re-establishment of New Testament Christianity.[4] The Jesus People were motivated eschatologically with a full expectation of the return of Jesus in their lifetime. There was an apocalyptic urgency affirming Käsemann's dictum "the apocalyptic is the mother of all theology."[5] They were generally counter-cultural, sought ecstatic experience such as visions, speaking in tongues, the gifts of the Holy Spirit, and believed in the power of prayer. David Di Sabatino says that first and foremost the JPM was centered on salvation through an experience of faith in Jesus Christ as the "one way" to receive reconciliation and relationship with God.[6]

Jesus People were Bible literalists. Donald Miller's study of the JPM in 1997 notes the difficulty of defining the diverse movement. Recalling conversations with Vineyard pastors says the Jesus People had a biblical orthodoxy with a twist. For example one Vineyard pastor recounted that when he read the Bible it meant what it said. If it said, "love your enemies" it meant love your enemies. Another Vineyard pastor acknowledged that he found miracles a difficulty but also saw there was a biblical mandate to pray for the sick and so he did. As a result he saw people healed. He could not explain why or how people were healed and even reported the anomaly that when his faith was lowest he saw the most healings.[7] The literal understanding of scripture was important to all the Jesus People groups.

Miller's survey of 3500 Christians in churches with roots in the JPM found that thirty-two percent read the Bible daily and twenty percent said they did so more than once a day. Twenty-five percent said they read the Bible two or three times a week.[8] In the survey Miller found 32 percent of respondents said the Bible was the "actual" Word of God and a preponderant 65 percent said it was the "inspired" Word of God.[9] Even though the tendency of Jesus People was to shun orthodoxy and be counter-cultural or even anti-intellectual they saw Bible reading as important.

Miller's study challenged his personal theological convictions. Earlier he had written *The Case for Liberal Christianity*. He wrote it at a time when mainline churches were losing members at an alarming rate. The JPM was long gone. He counted himself lucky to still be a Christian. In the 1990s he received a grant to study the rapid growth of non-mainline churches.[10]

His study included 200 interviews with leaders of the churches and movements (primarily Calvary Chapels, Vineyard churches and Hope Chapels). He attended 200 church events, took field notes and surveyed numerous groups of Christians. These churches he identified as "New Paradigm Churches (NPC)" and labeled members "new paradigm Christians."

These new paradigm Christians had an assumption "that the Bible contains the narratives for understanding how God relates to humans."[11] It was a faith he said was "verified empirically, as the Bible becomes validated in everyday life."[12] They saw that in the Bible people were healed and transformed morally by the leading of the Holy Spirit. They assumed that there was authority for them to see and experience the same things. "The Bible seems to assume authority for these individuals as they practice what it says and have prayers answered, see people healed, watch people being transformed morally, and experience the 'leading' of the Holy Spirit in their own lives."[13] Miller found himself in the midst of people who did not just talk about miracles, healing and casting out demons, they were doing it.

Richard Bustraan says his investigation of the JPM supports several claims. He says that the Jesus People should be untethered from the Fundamentalist label. The JPM shares its theological roots with both Evangelicalism and Pentecostalism but are distinct in their theological expression. The Pentecostalism of the JPM was more accommodating to variations of ecclesial (church) structure and their *praxis* contained a strong theological resemblance to American Pentecostalism in general.[14] Bustraan's conclusion is that theologically the JPM should be placed in the domain of American Pentecostalism.

These preliminary remarks establish a base line for the JPM and starting point for the theological and cultural identity of the CFM. The Prescott Foursquare Church in January of 1970 was a broken church. In the next twenty years certain principles were established within the CFM that remain important to the ministry. These were not unique to the CFM. The themes of evangelism, transformation, discipleship and church planting were important throughout the Jesus People era. Popular books and articles were written. Transformation, discipleship and church planting became core issues for the Christian Fellowship Ministry.

Transformation in its common understanding means change. When transformation is used as a noun it means one thing is derived from another. When transformation is used as a verb it means a thing undergoes a change of form or nature.[15] The Prescott Foursquare Church of 1970 was transformed from a broken institution and discouraged and possibly disillusioned congregation to one involved in discipleship and church planting.

The task of the church is to make disciples. This implies evangelism and conversion. Transformation requires a relationship between the disciple and the disciple maker. The relationship is a unique and vitally important one. Without it there can be no spiritual transformation or impartation of spiritual life into the disciple. Discipleship is meant to be a long-term, stable relationship that allows for spiritual growth and maturity—transformation. Research in sociology, psychology and human physiology support the importance of relationships. This is especially true in spiritual formation of new converts.

The popular book *Celebration of Discipline* by Richard Foster gave impetus and shape to what has come to be known as spiritual formation.[16] Jeffrey Greenman says that the consensus of 2000 years is that spiritual formation is a "transformation" of heart, mind and spirit. It cannot be pursued in isolation but takes place in "the community of faith."[17] "Spiritual formation is our continuing response to the reality of God's grace shaping us into the likeness of Jesus Christ, through the work of the Holy Spirit, in the community of faith for the sake of the world."[18] Jesus sends his witnesses into the world for the sake of the world and the genius of spiritual formation is in the capacity of a witness to be the salt of the earth and the light of the world. The witness is literally a city set on a hill.[19] Eugene Peterson says, "The great weakness of North American spirituality is that it is all about us: fulfilling our potential, getting in on the blessing of God, expanding our influence, finding our gifts, getting a handle on principles by which we can get an edge on the competition. And the more there is of us the less there is of God."[20] Greenman sees spiritual formation as a transformation that occurs in a faith community that encourages, mentors and brings persons to a place of accountability for the purpose of fulfilling the Great Command of loving God and our neighbors. God calls for a renewing of the mind (Rom. 12:1-2) and commands a radical love (Mark 12:30).[21] Spiritual formation is necessary to impact the world with the love of God. We are transformed to fulfill the Great Commission and the Great Commandment. These two are sometimes viewed as mutually exclusive but both are necessary for believers. We are transformed to make an impact on the world and not just for personal development.

In an analysis of the Vineyard Movement and spiritual formation, Vineyard missions expert Mark Fields and Vineyard pastor Stephen Summerell note that the spiritual formation of leaders will "ultimately contribute to the health and ongoing successes of the church's mission in the world."[22] The self-identification of the Vineyard Movement is that they are a church planting movement.[23] In Fields and Summerell's analysis they find the sustaining factor for ministers is that they pay attention to their spiritual formation.

> We have observed several points of intersection between personal spirituality and effective engagement in mission, two of which stand out. The first corollary is between a pursuit of spiritual formation and the potential for longevity in ministry and mission. When committed leaders consider leaving ministry due to burnout or lack of spiritual maturity, we have found one sustaining factor to be actively engaging in their own spiritual formation. The second is the importance of integrity, that as much as possible one's life mirrors the message one proclaims. Followers of Jesus are called to be good news not only share it.[24]

Fields and Summerell say the "ongoing response to the Holy Spirit" in the Greenman definition of spiritual formation is a disconnect for many. They see in some pastors a lack of connection between their understanding of God and what Jesus taught. Their idea of God does not connect with what Jesus taught and what the Bible teaches. Their lifestyle is then not connected to the biblical teaching.[25] "If leaders are struggling with caring for their own souls," Fields and Summerell continue, "what do we imagine they are modeling to those they lead?"[26] A minister can only lead by what and who they are.

Spiritual formation or the lack of spiritual formation in the inner person is mirrored in how a person lives.[27] The Vineyard definition of mission taken from Fuller Theological Seminary's Charles van Engen is about crossing barriers to reconcile non-faith persons to themselves, to one another and to God. Following repentance they are gathered into churches for spiritual transformation by the work of the Holy Spirit.[28] Individual transformation occurs in churches for the transformation of the church and the world. It is not simply about being a member or acknowledging a confession. Transformation is not just for gaining spiritual knowledge. As Greenman says, "the purpose of theology is formation of mission."[29]

David J. Bosch (1929-1992) can properly be described as a missionary-scholar. He was raised in South Africa and was a student during the height of the apartheid crisis. As a member of the Dutch Reformed Church in South Africa's Cape Province, a pro-apartheid Afrikaner, and believing that blacks were simply part of the natural environment, Bosch had a sort of conversion when teaching a Sunday service for blacks. It was a lasting discovery that many of those blacks were also Christians. Convinced of a call to Christian service and particularly the mission field, he became a divinity student. He received two degrees, one in languages and the other in theology. He also began to question the morality of apartheid.

After receiving his doctorate he became a Dutch Reformed Church (DRC) missionary to the Xhosa people in Transkei. His continued academic endeavor while a missionary distanced him from the mainstream DRC that still supported apartheid. He was denied a position as DRC professor in Pretoria because of it. Instead he took a position as professor of missiology at the University of South Africa in 1972 where he served until his untimely death in an automobile accident in 1992. His ability in language (Afrikaans, English, German, Dutch, French and Xhosa), his traditional Western education in Switzerland under Oscar Cullman and Karl Barth, and his South African heritage and mission work made him an international person. This allowed him to be a connection between the World Council of Churches, the Lausanne Committee and the World Evangelical Fellowship. He was, therefore, uniquely qualified to write *Transforming Mission*.[30]

*Transforming Mission* is Bosch's attempt to define mission in the current or contemporary world. He believes that this cannot be done without a firm grasp on the past twenty centuries of church, and in particular, mission history. He finds a crisis in missions he calls a malaise or failure of nerve in contemporary Christian enterprise. The crisis faced in missions is because of a series of interconnected cultural phenomena that includes the preeminence of science and technology, a de-Christianized West, an acute sense of guilt in the West, increasing disparity between the rich and poor, and a younger generation that does not accept the norms of the past.[31]

Bosch believes a grasp of the many "interim" definitions the church has held concerning evangelism and missions is necessary before any redefinition or transforming of mission is possible. The bulk of the text in *Transforming Mission* is a recounting of the history of missions. Bosch accomplishes this in two of the three main sections of the book covering about 60 percent of the text. The first of these sections covers the New Testament church. He treats the New Testament as a missiological document[32] with particular attention to Matthew and the Great Commission, Luke-Acts as the gospel to the rich and poor and the letters of Paul as invitation to the world to join God's community.

It was during the New Testament era that the church was finding itself as the unique community of God. That community, according to Bosch, is about evangelism or mission.[33] Matthew is a mandate for the conflicted early Christian community not yet separate from Judaism. Those who viewed the law as important to Christian living are in conflict with those who desired to live by the Spirit.[34] Matthew is not a passion story with a long introduction. It is a call for the church to be involved in the mission of God. In Luke Bosch sees liberation but it is not just from law but liberation to a new life. Luke writes to a second generation of Christians whose enthusiasm is flagging. They have not seen the *parousia* (Second Coming of Christ) as promised, and are increasingly hostile to the Jews.[35] Salvation of those 'outside' is an important theme for Luke.

Paul, Bosch summarizes, understood the church as a new community. It is an interim one that must be unique to accomplish its mission as a missionary community. Bosch, building on an earlier idea, sees Paul's theology as coming from his *praxis* rather than from his *theologia*. In other words, Paul's concept of the church came from his experience with God. It did not come from anyone else. Paul's evangelism (the "Mother of Theology")[37] gave rise to his theology of the church. The church is unlike any other community or group because of its distinctive nature in three arenas. 1) The righteousness of God is a gift to the church because individual believers do not exist in isolation. 2) The church language of belonging or kinship speaks to the transcendence of social and cultural barriers so all may belong. And 3) the church exists for the sake of the world. These mark the church as a unique social group unlike the Stoics, Epicureans or others.[38] Bosch is making the point that the church operates by conduct and not just by declaration or creedal membership. The preacher as a person backs the declaration of the gospel. It is conduct that comes by the work of the Holy Spirit transforming believers.

It is in the second section of *Transforming Mission* that Bosch introduces the theme of transformation as a paradigm shift. Thomas Kuhn's *The Structure of Scientific Revolutions* says a paradigm shift is a revolutionary change in thought. Bosch says the idea is relevant because we live in an era of change.[39] In a theological paradigm shift the old view does not completely disappear. It also possible in theological paradigm shifts something old might be rediscovered.[40]

By looking at cultures that more closely resemble the world of the New Testament a deeper understanding of transformation is possible. Paul Hiebert (1932-2007) was a professor of mission and anthropology, pastor and missionary in India. He was born in India to missionary parents and at his death was arguably the leading missiological anthropologist in America. Hiebert was able to fuse theology and anthropology in a unique and important way. He saw spiritual transformation as the work of God in sinners that makes them citizens of heaven.

Transformation is also a work of God in the church or community of God's people. Since it is a work of God we can see only vaguely the divine nature of transformation.[41] In his view people are called to respond to an invitation to leave their false gods, the self-idolatry of wealth, pride, sex, and race and return to God their Creator and Lord. When they respond they are transformed and their spiritual change has earthly consequences that take place in their concrete history. It is both an individual and corporate change because people do not live outside of their culture.[42] The transformation of Romans 12:2 is connected to a life of service in the church assembly (Romans 12:3-14).

Hiebert sees that the Western mind views people without the corporate or communal connection. They believe conversion is something people think or do individually. While verbally denying salvation by works this view ignores the work of God.[43] Hebrew thought, however, operates in extrinsic or relational categories that are important to one's understanding of transformation or conversion.[44] In other words, one cannot be transformed without a corresponding change or transformation in the person and circumstances of their life.

The Old Testament word and call to turn also implies a turn in relationship to persons and/or other things. Similarly the New Testament *metanoein* and *epistrephein* for conversion mean to turn around. Luke uses the more dynamic *epistrephein* and Paul uses *apostrephein* and *anastrephein* that in Greek carry a meaning of turning around and then walking. For Hiebert the more Hebrew and biblical view of transformation is both a point and a process. That is, it has a simple beginning of turning from wherever or whatever one is but it produces radical and lifelong consequences. Turning perhaps involves a minimal amount of information about Christ but changes one's relationship with him to a commitment to follow him in a lifelong series of decisions after an initial turning.[45] This view of transformation determines much about how we do missions. The mission of evangelism is far more than simply getting people to assent to particular truths.

When we begin to think about discipleship and church planting this becomes important to our understanding. This is illustrated in a mission project among African rainforest pygmies. Benno Van den Toren studied a work among pygmies in the Central African Republic that began in the 1950s. It appeared to have produced a number of churches with indigenous pastors. However, apart from the pastors and a few workers there was little growth and maturity in the converts. Mission work brought them to a confession of faith though they did not see themselves as sinners.

Without downplaying the importance of confession Van den Toren found that after confession of faith and baptism, new converts continued in traditional religion and practices that contradicted their Christian faith. What he discovered was a lack of discipleship and, importantly, the gospel they received did not relate to their everyday life. The confession was not based on conviction of sin or understanding of following Jesus. Confession was simply answering some questions that a Western missionary might ask.[46]

The pygmy converts understood a confession of faith was important—especially to the missionary—but were unable to translate that into a transformed lifestyle. The confession or point of turning was not meaningful to how they lived their lives. The confession "Jesus is Lord" must make sense in daily living.[47] In getting a confession many feel the work is done. But transformation individually and hence corporately in a church or culture must relate to the confessor's lifestyle.

The rainforest pygmy culture is simple. It is about survival. After generations of being abused and enslaved by other tribes they have a deep insecurity. Their traditional religion encourages additional gods and ancestors in their worship and Jesus is, to their thinking, a god like all the rest. They are pragmatic. Religion must pay immediate dividends. The Christian principle of patient endurance is difficult to understand in a culture of day-to-day survival. Family structure is also important. Respect in the family and in the community come by having a skill (hunting, fishing, building, etc.) that contributes to the entire community.[48] To further complicate the issue Bible translators used the name of a pygmy traditional god (*kamba*) as the name for the God of the Bible.[49] Transformation is not simply change and not simply a decision about words. The product of mission is a change in conduct that is meaningful individually and corporately. Everyone is a member of a community. Transformation of the community occurs as the members are transformed.[50]

Rodney Lambert is a missionary of the CFM in Vanuatu, South Pacific. Vanuatu is the former New Hebrides and has a history of cannibalism (of missionaries) and a strong tribal/family structure. He reports the dynamic of salvation affecting one member also affecting the whole of the family or tribe. In some cases he has witnessed when a king (leader of a tribal or extended family unit) prays to receive Jesus the impact is nearly immediate and the whole tribe responds. He is not necessarily saying that they all suddenly become Christians. He is noting the impact of one transformation on the whole.[51]

David Bosch said we live in an era of change. This makes the idea of "paradigm shift"[52] relevant, according to Bosch, for the "church and missions."[53] The JPM brought a paradigm shift into the religious atmosphere of American culture. It brought a contextualized gospel to a generation of young people. It was more than a confession. It brought a theology of *praxis*. It was not their father's religion. It was theirs. What they believed found its way into their everyday lives. Bosch says evangelism is the "mother of theology."[54] When Paul writes to the Romans he fuses his theology of how a human becomes right with God to how that person is then expected to act in living the life of a believer.

Making disciples is the commission of the church. This assures the faithful reproduction of the core content and character of the church that is the result of Jesus' commission to evangelize the nations. Dallas Willard in *The Great Omission* identifies the New Testament as, "a book about disciples, by disciples, and for the disciples of Jesus Christ."[55] He goes on, however, to lament the absence of real disciples, disciple making and discipleship in the church of today. The idea that we should make converts and sign them onto the rolls of church membership has subverted the process of making disciples. "Not having made our converts disciples, it is *impossible* [italics original] for us to teach them how to live as Christ lived and taught (Luke 14:26)."[56]

Chris Shirley says,

> "The word discipleship does not appear in the New Testament, the concept is implied through Jesus command in the Great Commission to make disciples."

Although discipleship has wide appeal and doctrinal credibility the place of the church is increasingly being criticized. Frank Viola and George Barna have documented a critical view of the church.[57] George Barna has prophesied the demise of the church into irrelevance as millions of attendees leave in favor of an alternative community. Barna estimates that at the turn of the century as many as twenty percent of Americans had a faith journey revolving around various cultural sources. This will increase to around thirty-five percent by 2025, leaving the local church as the primary means of spiritual "experience and expression" for only thirty to thirty-five percent of Americans.[58] He says "revolutionaries" are drawing people away from local congregations. "Theirs is a personal choice based on a genuine desire to be holy and obedient, but finding that need better served outside the framework of congregational structures."[59] Other prominent leaders such as Brian McLaren have expressed deep reservations about the church as it is currently conceived in the western world.[60] Reggie McNeal notes, "The single most challenging cultural shift facing many spiritual leaders involves the huge reorientation away from the church, a shift that has accelerated since the late 1980s."[61]

To their credit McLaren, Barna and McNeal are concerned for the faith once delivered to the saints. Nonetheless, the church is the vital structure for spiritual formation and therefore discipleship. In *Transforming Discipleship*, Greg Ogden quotes the late Ray Stedman, "The Life of Jesus is still being manifest among people, but now no longer through an individual physical body, limited to one place on earth, but through a complex, corporate body called the church."[62] Ogden himself says, "The Scriptures picture the church as an essential, chosen organism in whom Christ dwells; the reality is that people view the church as an optional institution, unnecessary for discipleship."[63] Chris Shirley argues the church is not irrelevant but required for making disciples. "What I would argue … is that the local church is the biblically-ordained and relevant vehicle for transformational discipleship."[64] The word disciple means being an adherent of someone, some teaching or some philosophy. Discipleship implies being in a process of formation. Shirley says, "I would suggest that formation is the result of discipleship" and "although the word discipleship does not appear in the New Testament, the concept is implied through Jesus command in the Great Commission to make disciples."[65]

James C. Wilhoit argues that the process of spiritual formation takes place through the commonness of the community Christ has established, the church. He comments in his opening chapter, "Spiritual formation is *the* [emphasis in original] task of the church. Period." and "The church was formed to form. Our charge, given by Jesus himself, is to make disciples."[66] He goes on to lament the "disquieting trend" that so many have "settled for secondary goals" that do not produce spiritually healthy disciples.[67] Spiritual activity is taking place but it is not making disciples of Jesus Christ. Rather it is producing a "mediocre product."[68]

As important as the church community is to the discipleship process, it is not the only ingredient in discipleship. The relationship of the twelve to Jesus was of obvious importance to their spiritual formation. H. Usener in *Organisation der Wissenschaft* noted,

It has long been recognized that the Gk. philosophical schools both at the time of their formation and in the manner of their operation were working fellowships under the decisive leadership of the master who formed their centre. There are also important reasons for assuming that this was true from the very first, and not just from the time of Plato and Aristotle.[69]

From the beginning, then, there was an attachment of the disciple to a disciple maker.

The almost technical sense of the word [disciple], which implies a direct dependence of the one under instruction upon an authority superior in knowledge, and which emphasizes [sic] the fact that this relation cannot be dissolved, controls the whole usage, no matter whether the reference is to the winning of technical or academic information and skill.[70]

In the first century discipleship was a common methodology for the formation of life in students of a master.

"Antiquity knows the master-disciple in two forms. The first is in the sphere of philosophical culture, the second in that of cultic and religious activity. The two forms come together where philosophical and religious elements intersect in the person of the master. This may be seen at the time of early Christianity."[71]

Attachment and loss might be considered a relatively new field of study. It came about as an extension of ideas about motivational drives in humans. The idea that humans are moved by the physiological drives of sex, nourishment and warmth dominated psychology until the publication of *King Solomon's Ring* by Konrad Lorenz.[72] Lorenz noted the additional motivational factor of relationships. He found that growth and maturity were related to relational attachment. Desmond Morris[73] and E. O. Wilson[74] published popular books placing the framework of animal growth and maturity onto human social patterns. The primary pioneer in the field of attachment was John Bowlby. According to Mario Mikulincer and Philip R. Shaver, he "borrowed from ethology the concept of a behavioral system." It effectively organized "survival responses of an organism to changing environmental factors."[75] In other words attachment was important for growth and social development. The concept of attachment is important in discipleship because the attachment figures "are not just close, important relationship partners," rather, "they are special individuals to whom a person turns when protection and support are needed."[76] The definition of an attachment figure would narrow down to a close relationship partner that is a "secure base."[77] The disciple maker is a secure base or reference point for development and growth.

Most of the studies done by Bowlby and his successors were with children. The language of attachment theory reflects that pioneering work. However, the field has opened up and numerous studies dealing with adult relationships have been conducted. The field of romantic partners has certainly become a fruitful one. Other adult relationships have been studied, however, and are applicable to the relationship between the disciple maker and the disciple. This relationship is the necessary one for spiritual transformation.

A. B. Bruce's *The Training of the Twelve*, first published near the end of the nineteenth century begins by pointing out the difficulty of discovering how discipleship came about.

> All beginnings are more or less obscure in appearance, but none were ever more obscure than those of Christianity. What an insignificant event in the history of the church, not to say the world, this first meeting of Jesus of Nazareth with five humble men, Andrew, Peter, Philip, Nathanael, and another unnamed! It actually seems almost too trivial to find a place even in the evangelic narrative. For we have here to do not with any formal solemn call to the great office of apostleship, or even with the commencement of an uninterrupted discipleship, but at the utmost with the beginnings of an acquaintance with and of faith in Jesus on the part of certain individuals who subsequently became constant attendants on His person, and ultimately apostles of His religion. Accordingly we find no mention made in the three first gospels of the events here recorded.[78]

Bruce calls the earliest disciples five "humble men" but that is reading much into the story. These soon to be disciples had issues similar to the ones faced in our generation. It seems reasonable to assume something akin to modern day issues in the disciples because of the biblical truth of the commonality of humankind: "No temptation has seized you except what is common to man (1 Cor. 10:13)." Biblically, the issues of the fall, the image of God, the dignity and destiny of humankind all apply universally. The images of the Twelve in the gospels tell us they were fearful, prone to peer pressure, prejudiced, uncomprehending, ambitious and argumentative as much as any person today. At least one was not just capable of betrayal but actually carried it out.

We also know some specifics. We know the fishing contingent among the disciples was at least part of the time unsuccessful and even discouraged with their production. We know that at least one of the disciples, Simon the Zealot, was a political malcontent, an ex-zealot of a rebel named Judas whose political ambitions were the overthrow of the Roman government adopting the watchword, "We have no Lord or Master but God."[79] We know of another disciple that must have experienced the rejection of his brethren. He was a publican or tax collector. Collecting taxes for the occupying Roman government was a despised occupation. The Jews considered such work tantamount to being a traitor. Matthew was one of three Publicans to come to Jesus and he became one of the Twelve. Simon and Matthew come from opposite poles of the social scale. One worked for the Roman government and the other vowed to take it apart by force. The irony was not lost on Bruce.

> It gives me pleasant surprise to think of Simon the zealot and Matthew the publican, men coming from so opposite quarters, meeting together in close fellowship in the little band of twelve. In the persons of these two disciples extremes meet— the tax-gatherer and the tax-hater: the unpatriotic Jew, who degraded himself by becoming a servant of the alien ruler; and the Jewish patriot, who chafed under the foreign yoke, and sighed for emancipation.[80]

Bruce was disturbed, however, by the idea that these twelve are considered by some to be "all but useless."[81] In defending the Twelve's character he notes they were obscure but not useless. Not all became Peters or Johns and thankfully there was a diversity of gifts. Again Bruce says, we cannot simply assume because there are so few facts.[82] John MacArthur calls them "twelve ordinary men[83] and William Barclay simply calls them "Chosen."[84] But "unschooled, ordinary men (Acts 4:13)" does not mean they were more susceptible to sin, vices and failure. They were definitely not useless. Scripture does at least tell us they were people with the same kinds of issues that press upon every generation.

The presence of Matthew and Simon the Zealot in the apostolic band tells us at a minimum that Jesus discipleship was able to connect with a diversity of people with varying degrees and kinds of human problems. It is not just the diversity of the apostolic band that informs us of Jesus ministry. Jesus ministry also encountered women. Some were considered the dregs of society such as Mary Magdalene, the woman at the well in Samaria and a woman caught in adultery. Jesus also encountered some of the elite of society such as Nicodemus (John 3) and Joseph of Arimathea (John 19:38). These encounters show us clearly Jesus was not entrenched in making categorical assumptions about people. In all of these events there was a possibility of becoming a follower of Jesus. Not everyone responded well but Jesus was able to communicate effectively and lead him or her to decisions vital to life. In contrast the Pharisees and religious schools of that era were exclusive. Jesus was inclusive, not exclusive.

William Willimon says, "Picture this: Would I begin a homiletics class by saying, 'The goal of this class is for you to imitate me?'" He continues, "No. It strikes us as the height of conceit."[85] But, this is exactly the issue of discipleship as Jesus did it. His call to discipleship was to follow him and be like him."[86] Willimon relates, "At a faculty retreat a few years ago, one of my colleagues asked, 'Does it bother any of you that some of our students are sexually promiscuous, that some are indulging in self-destructive and addictive practices?'"[87] He uses the question to make a basic but profound point about discipleship. Paul makes it clear. To the Corinthians he writes, "Even though you have ten thousand guardians in Christ, you do not have many fathers, for in Christ Jesus I became your father through the gospel. Therefore I urge you to imitate me (1 Cor. 4:15-16 NIV)." Paul is contrasting the teacher relationship (translated "guardians") with that of being a follower ("imitate me") and then adds, "For this reason I am sending to you Timothy, my son, whom I love, who is faithful in the lord. He will remind you of my way of life in Christ Jesus, which agrees with what I teach everywhere in every church (1 Cor. 4:17 NIV)." These statements go beyond a student-teacher relationship. There is an invitation to be like the teacher. To the Philippians Paul invites them to, "Join with others in following my example, brothers, and take note of those who live according to the pattern we gave you (Phil. 3:17)." In other words, Paul's life agrees with what he teaches.

To the Thessalonians Paul uses the verb *mimeomai* to describe their experience in the gospel. "You became imitators of us and the Lord; in spite of severe suffering, you welcomed the message with the joy given by the Holy Spirit (1 Thessalonians 1:6 NIV)" and, "For you brothers, became imitators of Christ's churches in Judea, which are in Christ Jesus: You suffered from your own countrymen the same things those churches suffered from the Jews, who killed the Lord Jesus … (1 Thess. 2:14-15 NIV)." And the same verb is used in Hebrews 6:12, "We do not want you to become lazy, but to imitate those who through faith and patience inherit what has been promised." W. E. Vine says this word is always used in a good sense and in a continuous form signaling a definitive act in the past (conversion) and teaches that what we became at conversion we must continue to be "thereafter."[88]

In this New Testament language we have something far greater and more important than a casual relationship, common acquaintance, teacher-student relationship, or a master-slave relationship. There is uniqueness to the disciple maker-disciple relationship. The father-son language in contrast to pedagogue-student language tells us something akin to a genetic transfer of life occurs. It is not simply transferring of the pedagogue's notes onto the notebooks of the students. Willimon's point is that until we are willing to say we want you to be 'like' us we are really just asking the students to take good notes, study hard, and pass the exams. This may relieve the teacher or professor of responsibility for the student's behavior but it is not discipleship. Disciples are not being transformed today because they are not required to do so.

The issue for Willimon is the product of the church—the disciple of Christ. What does the church produce? "For the little band of Christians at Philippi, constantly in danger of seduction by the majority pagan culture, there was no better textbook than the lives of those who bore the burden of leadership. Discipleship still depends on identifying examples, saints, people worthy of imitation."[89] It is important to note, "The world is quite right in judging Christianity by the lives it produces. Lacking changed lives we pervert the gospel into a cerebral exercise. But Christianity is a lifestyle, the following of someone headed in a direction one would not normally go."[90] Discipleship is about following the Christian life of another person. We learn best by following an example. Willimon uses the example of learning to ride a horse. "One learns to ride a horse by watching someone who is good at riding, by being led step-by-step by that person, and by imitating her moves."[91]

Paul Hiebert, long term missiologist and missions writer, tells the South Indian proverb of the banana and the banyan. He points out that in South India there are huge trees that dot the landscape. These banyans grow to tremendous stature and elegance. Air roots drop to the ground; they develop secondary trunks and buttresses to support their massive size. They become so massive that they cover as much as an acre of real estate. Birds nest in them. Animals and humans find shade and protection there. An entire ecosystem can reside in, on, and among their branches and shade. At the same time there are bananas that grow not as tall but bear a popular fruit. The uniformity of the banana's ecosystem supports few species. However, while the banyan is spreading its huge branches, while it is building the buttresses that support its massive size and while it is dropping down its air roots for nourishment, the banana within six months begins to put out new sprouts that begin to grow. Within six months these sprouts are putting out new sprouts. At eighteen months bananas appear on the original plant. Meanwhile the other sprouts are continuing the cycle. The difference between the banana and the banyan, however, comes at death. When the banyan dies it leaves a barren landscape. The nutrients of the soil have been used. Nothing has grown within its sphere of influence. Its shade has been too dominant to allow anything else to take root or grow beneath its branches and the ecosystem it supported has to move on. Life that depended on the banyan must find another shelter or perish from exposure. The banana, on the other hand, has produced dozens of additional banana trees. A transfer of life from generation to generation has occurred. The Indian proverb says, "Nothing grows under a banyan tree."[92]

Hiebert uses the illustration to contrast leadership styles. Many very good leaders have great ministries but when they pass from the scene there are no leaders to step into their shoes. This is the core of discipleship for Hiebert. It is not merely imitation nor is it mere following. There must be transformation. Discipleship is about transformation. As Hiebert points out, "It is gratifying to train followers. They are an appreciative audience and make us feel important. They imitate our ways. They do not challenge our thinking or go beyond our teaching." He says, "It is easy to train followers. We decide what they should learn and how they should learn it."[93] Indeed the making of disciples is a different matter than gathering a crowd or getting people to be followers or imitators. There must be inward transformation that matches the outward conformity.

The training of leaders (disciples who will make disciples) is "less rewarding for our egos."[94] These people are transformed and carry the DNA, so to speak, of what has made the disciple maker a disciple maker. The disciple maker must involve disciples in real tasks. They must have real ministry and have the potential and possibility of failing. Hiebert points out that this process of training leaders produces transformation at every level of their life and lifestyle. "Spouses who encourage their husbands … to be leaders develop family styles of mutual submission. Parents who build their children as leaders begin early to teach them to think."[95] And the same goes for pastors and disciple makers who encourage and challenge: they establish strong churches that survive crisis and produce strong leaders.

Paul's contrast of father and pedagogue, Willimon's insight into teaching that produces examples for the world, and Hiebert's comparison of leaders and followers, all point to a unique relationship in the Kingdom of God between the disciple maker and the disciple. It is a relationship that begins at some point and continues through the ministry of the pastor and the disciple. Discipleship also involves a healing process. Many converts have past relationship issues that have left them wounded. These wounds hinder the formation of relationships that are necessary for discipleship. Neil Anderson, in his book *Discipleship Counseling*, after dealing with how to overcome bitterness, rebellion, habitual sin and a number of other issues comes to the issue of ancestral sin. Ancestral sin is the idea that something spiritual is transmitted from generation to generation. He says, "The last issue that needs to be resolved is ancestral sins that are passed on from one generation to another ... This is a crucial step for those people who come from dysfunctional families or families involved in cults or the occult."[96]

He is talking about former attachments that hinder an attachment to God and an attachment to a pastor or disciple maker. Can sin be inherited? Anderson answers, "No, but dispositions (genetic, environmental and spiritual)" may be. He points to Jeremiah 32:17-18: "[You] ... bring the punishment for the father's sins into the laps of their children after them." Anderson comments that Jesus does not let the generation that rejects him miss this lesson (Matt. 23.32, 34-36).[97] Attachments have a profound effect on life.

The relationship between the pastor/leader (disciple maker) and the disciple is unique and vitally important to personal success. Paul Stanley and Robert Clinton found after reviewing the lives of 600 leaders that most do not end well.

> Research on mid-career, contemporary leaders led to another conclusion—other individuals helped most of these men and women in timely situations along the way. We do not yet know if they will finish well, but their relationship to another person significantly enhanced their development. Most case studies listed three to ten significant people who helped shape their lives. And what is true of these leaders is also true of us.[98]

Their research focused on mentoring but it certainly fits discipleship. Richard Nixon spent most of his post-presidency career writing about politics. In *Leaders* he writes about his experiences with many of the leaders throughout the world. He makes a point about transitions similar to the point of Hiebert's Indian proverb. About Churchill's return to power at 76 years of age Richard Nixon writes, "It was also assumed he would turn over the reigns to his chosen successor, Anthony Eden. But for ... an old man, [giving up power and position] can be the same as giving up life itself."[99] He goes on to comment that De Gaulle, Churchill and Adenauer all had trouble allowing a successor and, in fact, put down those destined to succeed them.[100] "It is a truism of leadership that great leaders rarely groom younger men because they are so captivated by their own accomplishments that they cannot imagine anyone taking their places."[101] Douglas MacArthur was a notable exception. His post war appointee Shigeru Yoshida led Japan to fruitful policies that extended from 1957 to 1972 through his successors Nobusuke Kishi, Hayato Ikeda, and Eisaku Sato. The last two were graduates of the Yoshida School.[102] MacArthur and Yoshida were men who trained leaders. They discipled them so that what was in them became part of what was in their successors. Relationships are vital in every arena of life from political to spiritual. Destiny and transformation are tied to the relationships of a disciple. The disciple-maker and disciple relationship is the hinge for all that the New Testament church will accomplish.

# 4
# THERE WAS A HUNGER

*"The church is not ready to depend exclusively upon the gospel."*
Rene Padilla

The New Testament records the missionary activities of Paul that resulted in new churches. It appears obvious that church planting is part of the mission of God and that the church should be involved. The Director of the School of Cross-Cultural Mission of the Sydney Missionary and Bible College (Sydney, Australia) Richard Yates Hibbert writes, "Church planting, while not the ultimate goal of mission, is the primary means of bringing in the blessings of the kingdom."

He continues,

> In summary, both the church and kingdom are brought about by *missio Dei*, preaching the kingdom seems to be a synonym for evangelism and church planting, and although the kingdom is the final goal of God's mission, the church is the way and means by which he is accomplishing that purpose now.[1]

In the gradually unfolding revelation of the New Testament Hibbert sees church planting as implied in the Great Commission. "Under the influence of the Holy Spirit, churches appear as the natural consequence, and God's intended result of proclaiming the gospel."[2] The Antioch church provides a model for churches and was the focal point for the critical decision to allow incorporation of Gentiles in the churches.[3] The planting of churches has been a characteristic of missions since the apostolic age.[4]

Stuart Murray has directed church planting and evangelism at Spurgeon's College and developed a Church Planting course for Baptist and other ministers. He is deeply involved in city ministries. He writes that though you can argue that the facts of church planting speak for themselves and no biblical foundation is needed there is still a demand for one. "The subject of church planting ... is peripheral rather than central in the New Testament, whereas the kingdom of God is arguably the central theme of Jesus teaching and the integrating paradigm for the mission of the church."[5] The terms church planting, evangelism, mission and discipleship are many times used interchangeably or almost as synonyms. Other times they are used in conjunction with mission in such a way as to reduce mission to one defining element. Mission is not just soul winning. Mission is not just proclamation. As Murray expresses it, mission is not just a "recruitment drive."[6] It is obedience to the will of God and God's purposes. Hibbert and Murray both see the church and discipleship as necessary to the mission of God. Jesus loves the church, gave his life for her and calls her his bride (Eph. 5:23-27). Jesus has established the church as his work on the earth (Matt. 16:18).

Hibbert summarizes the necessity of community. Acceptance by God means acceptance by the church (Rom. 15.7 and Phil. 4:2-3). It is when believers are together they can grasp the love of God and know that all are branches of the same vine, building, and body of Christ. Jesus called the disciples to fellowship and to follow in solidarity with him (1 John 1:1-3).[7] Acts of justice and kindness cannot have impact unless they occur in the context of the church community.[8] It is hard to be obedient to Christ's command to love one another when there is not another. Random acts of kindness apart from connection with the local church, however good, remain random and unconnected with the love of God. Local churches are a tangible expression of the heavenly kingdom of God and the reality God uses to make known his manifold wisdom (Eph. 3:10).

Church planting is a reality of the New Testament. Hibbert uses the Malphurs definition of church planting as a "planned process of beginning and growing new local churches."[9] The controversy comes into play when the functional aspects or expression of mission are considered. The former editor of *Christianity Today* and prolific writer Carl F. H. Henry pointed out the tension confronting the modern church.

Perhaps no problem has distressed the modern churches more than determining the legitimacy of claims made upon Christian loyalties by champions of personal evangelism on the one hand and by those who call the church to social involvement on the other. These tensions now vex the church as never before in history. Carl Henry says, "The tension between personal religion and social engagement is not, of course, characteristic of every movement or ideology."[10] Without playing down either side he notes that God's desire in the New Testament is both personal and societal. God seeks to extend his kingdom and holy purpose throughout the creation.[11]

In the Old Testament the question was how personal holiness is preserved in the midst of national culture. In the New Testament the question is about the affect of socio-political thought on personal religion. In the Hebrew theocracy the question was how one maintains a vital personal relationship with God. In our modern/postmodern era of individuality the question is how to promote social change through the church and not governments.[12] Henry traces the tension to three issues. Modernism was objectionable to churches first because it sacrificed the transcendence nature of God and forfeited the miracle dimension of Christianity. Modernism and liberal theology, however, view social change in terms of evolution. History was evolving and those of a non-evangelical persuasion viewed humankind as good. Second, this caused a reaction in Protestant Fundamentalism that asserted the necessity of a new birth. Third, many seeking social involvement aligned themselves with a socialist worldview. The result was a withdrawal of churches from social constructs or a social interest that was motivated only as far as an evangelistic by-product.[13] Carl Henry was concerned about this dynamic in 1947 when he wrote *The Uneasy Conscience of Modern Fundamentalism*.[14] Henry's 1972 paper was written at the height of the JPM that was becoming untethered from fundamentalism. It was a time of reasserting conservative Christianity but Jesus People were largely socially liberal. Henry's plea was that young people could be challenged to seek social justice. This was also a time when liberation theologies were challenging the religious environment.

The tension remains today. Paul had to remind the early Christians that their personal salvation and relationship to God did not negate the importance of God's just purposes.[15] Rodney Stark's sociological research finds the importance of God's justice in the light of first century evangelism and church planting. The truly revolutionary aspect of Christianity lay in moral imperatives such as "Love one's neighbor as oneself," "Do unto others as you would have them do unto you," "It is more blessed to give than to receive," and "When you did it to the least of my brethren, you did it unto me."[16] The inconsistent behavior of the gods and goddesses of the pagan world could not motivate the ethical behavior Christianity generated. The cities of the New Testament world were rife with crime and sickness, subject to natural disaster and social chaos. This made Christianity radically different and a source of moral power in the pagan world of the first and second centuries.[17] The abandonment of Christianity today threatens to also remove the moral power it generates in society.

Society can provide many things for its citizens but it cannot provide salvation and meaning in life. The two starting points of worldviews today are incompatible. One side starts with the belief that humankind is basically good from the start and inequality of whatever kind distorts that basic goodness. The other side starts with the fundamental understanding that humankind is bent toward sin. Sin then demands a payment price that is provided only by the blood of Jesus. It is wrong to assume that viewing humans as sinners precludes concern for social justice. In many ways healthy congregations support the weak, the infirm, the destitute and those who find themselves alone in life. Healthy congregations practice true religion (James 1:27).

The church is God's agent in evangelism and it is the nature of the church to grow and reproduce.[18] Paul W. Chilcote and Laceye C. Warner note the overlap of terms regarding church planting, church growth and evangelism. They affirm that evangelism is the heart of church mission and it is also the core of ecclesiastical (church) practice.[19] Evangelism occurs in the midst of numerous church practices such as administration, education, pastoral care, worship and hospitality. Though evangelism occurs among these many interconnected practices it remains a core component of discipleship and church planting.[20]

God has shown himself to be a God of pattern and purpose. Moses was divinely provided a pattern of heavenly things and told to build a tabernacle according to the plan shown him (Exod. 26:30, Heb. 8:5). Paul wrote to the Philippians, "Dear brothers and sisters, pattern your lives after mine, and learn from those who follow our example (Phil. 3:17 NLT)." We are not free to change the pattern of life God ordained simply because we believe circumstances or cultures have changed. The biblical admonition is "Do not remove the ancient landmark which your fathers have set (Prov. 22:28 NKJV)." As mentioned, the JPM believed they were setting in place New Testament Christianity. God has established boundaries and patterns for life as believers and also for churches. In Athens Paul reasoned God "has made from one blood every nation of men to dwell on all the face of the earth, and has determined their pre-appointed times and the boundaries of their dwellings, so that they should seek the Lord, in the hope that they might grope for Him and find Him (Acts 17:26-27 NKJV)."

In a critical analysis of Christianity at the Symposium on Evangelism, Rene Padilla says the church can adopt a configuration that is not suitable for revival. Padilla discusses how the Latin American church has been co-opted by consumer society. He says that today the basic questions of human life cannot be discussed and Christianity cannot count on help from society at large to maintain and pass Christian values on to others. He says that today being a Christian is for a heroic minority. Pastoral work now vacillates between ministry to a minority of true believers or to a mass of falsely committed "consumer" Christians. The demands of discipleship are reduced to a minimum.[21] The pastoral minister lives in fear that if the true minority becomes the focus of pastoral energy then the uncommitted majority will be surrendered to the world. Padilla says, "The church is not ready to depend exclusively upon the gospel."[22]

The current atmosphere and culture of the world has reduced the gospel to simply a message. It is a spiritual message to be sure but it is still just a message. It is a message that says all that is necessary is to accept Jesus as an all-sufficient Savior. This separates Jesus as Savior from Jesus as Lord. Churches can count people for the sake of statistics on a bare minimum of confession or they can count Christians on the basis of the committed, engaged, and genuinely involved.[23] "The church has only two alternatives in its confrontation with the world: either it adapts itself to the world and betrays the Gospel, or it responds to the Gospel and enters into conflict with the world."[24]

Walter Brueggemann says the core task is to take a confrontational tone against alien spiritual powers. He says the quarrel between evangelization and social action is cheap and uninformed.[25] Commenting on Jesus sending the disciples as sheep among wolves (Matt. 10:16-20), he says they will evoke deep hostility and be in trouble with those in authority as a normal state.[26] It is understood that the intention of God sending disciples into the world is for the creation of an alternative community in the midst of conventional and non-transformed communities.[27] The gospel penetrates hostile environments when proclaimed in the power of the Holy Spirit. However, our culture is reluctant to proclaim or adhere to that proclamation. Bosch claims the disciples were equally reluctant and did mission as a result of an "inner law of their lives" obtained at Pentecost.[28] "Our culture seems to take the position that believing deeply in the tenets of one's faith represents a kind of mystical irrationality [persons] would do better to avoid."[29]

Padilla sees the issues and conflicted character of many churches. It is not the pattern of unity that Christ and the New Testament advocate. The biblical pattern is not a western, eastern, Latino, or African liturgical one. The New Testament drama informs us that proclamation of the gospel results in converts, disciples, and new churches. Six times the Book of Acts documents that the churches or disciples were multiplied. The New Testament also informs us that it brings conflict with entrenched religious, political, and social power structures. The gospel is more than a confrontation with a disbelieving culture. It is a confrontation with personal sin. It is easier to see evil as something inherent in human systems, government, capitalism, industrialization, or organizations. Evil is in the world both individually and corporately. It is not merely systemic. It is personal.

> To think of evil as only systemic is erroneous, just as it is wrong for us to consider evil as only personal. Evil is headed by the devil, and he has legions. He is able to affect and infect individuals because he has the raw material with which to work—sinners ... Individuals who are infected also infect society as they submit to the schemes of the devil (Eph. 6:11). Christians are in a battle, a fight ... especially those on the front line.[30]

Andrew Blackwood, the Presbyterian minister, also understood the difficulty of presenting the gospel in a hostile environment. It is the issue of personal sin that triggers resistance and argument or even a battle.

The minister must deal with souls, and, however sensitive, the issue of sin. He represents men before God and God before men ... Sin means wrong relations or lack of right relations. This "lack of rightness" involves wrong relations with others and with in man himself. This is what makes ministry difficult—people have "sin" in relation to others as well as to God ... Here is an issue with much unavailing prayer because to come to the presence of God means we must deal with issues of sin. Sin that so easily besets us ... and separates us from God.[31]

Jesus is a counter-cultural Christ.[32] "To say that sin is personal ... is not to say that its consequences are limited to the individual ... On the contrary, that which is personal is intrinsically related to that which is collective ... Every personal action affects the community. Personal sin brings with it collective guilt."[33] This was the story of Israel's conquest of Jericho and Aachan's sin of stealing the spoil that belonged to God.

Clearly there is much wrong with the evangelical church world. Competition for finances and market share in a consumer society are evils to be reckoned with. Nonetheless a reactionary approach will not see biblical Christianity any more than a laissez faire attitude about the evils of the church world. Jesus said he would build his church. Just claiming that two or three gathered together is a church falls short of the definition of a church. The church has distinctive marks that make it a church. A sign over the door admittedly does not make it Christian or a church. Churches preach the gospel, keep the commands of baptism and a community meal remembering the Lord, and hold their members accountable for the testimony of Christ. Churches are gatherings of the redeemed people of God, called out of the world to hear from God and receive direction for their lives.

The local church possesses the incredible reality of the Christian experience. Christianity is about relationships. It is not some cloud of theological jargon but a group of people who know each other, meet regularly to hear from God, and enjoy Jesus and each other's presence.

Jesus walks among these actual believers. The church sets the course of society. This assembly, the local church, is afforded incredible dignity and has the wherewithal to accomplish God's purposes and destiny on the earth. Neither the mega-church with thousands of members nor the small church of a few members is unseen and unimportant to God. God is at work in these churches (congregations) to bring about his harvest, bring disciples to maturity, and to raise the resources necessary both financially and in personnel to accomplish His will. The church is the logical result of evangelism and the preaching of the gospel. If you want to make the Christian experience real, make it local. Or, put another way, if you want to contextualize the gospel and the Christian experience, make it local. Make it work with real people in real time in real locations. The local church has responsibilities in God's purposes. It exists to send.

The first responsibility of the local church is reaping the harvest. The responsibility of the local congregation is to make the presence of God known on the local level. The church is a colony of heaven. The truth, the light of the gospel, is to shine as light in the present age. The local congregation is a model of the self-propagating, self-sustaining, and self-governing kingdom of God. It is the pattern of things in heaven.

The second responsibility of the local church is the training of workers, leaders, and ministers. Discipleship occurs within an assembly of believers. Disciples in the local assembly are given genuine ministry. They have opportunity to deal with living souls, with real-life problems, and with real-life consequences. It is the local church that raises, recognizes and launches disciples in ministry. "Too often a headquarters mentality exists."[34] The sermons and programs come from headquarters but the local minister's circumstances may or may not have something to do with what headquarters demands. Paul and Barnabas were recognized and sent from the local congregation in Antioch (Acts 13).

The third task of the local assembly is the financing of the gospel. Self-support is a powerful spiritual issue. When Raymond Bakke established a work in Chicago he made two decisions. One, the ministers were those in the pews. It was a lay ministry. This is the heart of the New Testament church. All are ministers.[35] Second, he decided he was not working for free. It was important for the people in the pews to support the work of the ministry.

"I could not pastor people who were not paying me, because that would have been turning my back on them. Their powerlessness would have been reinforced if their pastor had been paid by and accountable to outsiders."[36]

Churches that fulfill these tasks are truly indigenous. Talking about urban ministry Conn and Ortiz try to define the word indigenous. "[W]hen we speak of indigenous leaders we mean those raised up in an urban [local] context in a particular cultural and sociological milieu, who consider this context their own, psychologically and sociologically. Indigenous leaders find the city home, they have no ties … that they have to overcome to remain in this urban setting."[37] An indigenous church is very much like that. It has been established in a sociological, psychological and cultural context that is home. This is the logical and best training ground for leaders. They know the people, the hardships, the limitations, the lifestyle, and the sense of destiny they all share. Biologically, indigenous simply means from within. From within the local congregation come the harvest of souls, the disciples and ministers, and the resources for accomplishing God's will.

Reflecting on the church and culture, Alan and Debra Hirsch say "The fact is that you can't be a disciple without being a missionary: no mission, no discipleship. It's that simple."[38] Alan is the director of Forge Ministries Training Network and Debra is involved with the church-planting agency Christian Associates International. They continue saying, "What we have gained in relevancy we lose in witness. … Though popular culture holds tremendous potential for good, unfortunately today's trend is toward a diversionary, mindless, celebrity-driven superficiality."[39]

The aim of church planting is the perpetuation of disciples. It is not the perpetuation of a program. Fads, programs, heresies, and structures come and go. The local church remains. History lets us see what happens when the local church stops producing disciples and planting churches. In modern Turkey one can visit the "sites" of the seven churches of Revelation. What is stunning is nearly the entire nation of Turkey today is Moslem, not Christian. This is the region Paul ministered in. The churches built by Christians are in ruins or they have been converted into mosques. The largest Christian structure in the ancient world was a church built in Constantinople (modern Istanbul). It was for many years a mosque and is now a museum of Moslem history. The perpetuation of disciples is not the same as academic instruction.

It certainly has a doctrinal component but it is an impartation of life from faith to faith. Making the gospel real to a local population or community is the aim of pioneering.

Walter Brueggemann says that discipleship and church planting are not about recruitment.

> It is the character, reality, will, and purpose of God that propels us into a crisis of discipleship and evangelism. The dominant script of our society wants to silence the voice of this God of miracle and imperative. Where the dominant script succeeds in eliminating God, moreover, the possibility of discipleship and the capacity for evangelism evaporate, because it is only the option of the good news that produces ground and opportunity for either discipleship or evangelism.[40]

The God who sends, sends with a compelling authority.[41] It is not just a nice idea of membership and learning. "It entails a resituating of our lives." The church has a negative issue with the world—the world is false. The church has a positive issue—God is "back in town."[42]

Transformation, discipleship and church planting are crucial to the purposes of God. Through these the gospel is made a visible and viable reality to a world that is antagonistic or ignorant of the goodness of God.

The data from the research can be organized along the idea of a pattern that is established, a pattern followed and a pattern that works. It is important to understand that a pattern is not the same thing as a program. The word pattern conjures up ideas of rigidity and uniformity. That can certainly be the case. The author's first job in a machine shop was bending piano wire to a certain shape. It was for a part that went into airplane seats. That is probably why no airplane seat is comfortable. The pattern was on a jig and pulling a handle bent the wire. Every piece was the same.

But there is another kind of pattern. It is living. While in Cambridge, England the author and his wife were able to visit the site where Francis Crick announced the structure of DNA. The genius of DNA is in its pattern. It is very simple and remarkably uniform. Nonetheless it is a pattern that allows for the wide diversity of seven-and-a-half billion humans. In another arena pilots follow what is called a pattern when approaching an airport to land. They follow a checklist before taking off or landing. It was a distraction that caused the MD-80 pilots to skip a portion of their checklist while getting ready to takeoff from Detroit's airport. They had failed to set the flaps before takeoff and crashed killing all on board except a two-year old. Likewise, a breakdown of the pattern of the DNA in a person can trigger catastrophic changes in a human life.

The biblical term pattern encompasses both the idea of rigidity and adaptability. The biblical pattern for revival has long been established. There are boundaries or landmarks that define the borders or parameters of church activity—individually and corporately—that God honors by his Spirit with revival.

Donald Miller looked for "triggers" in his research of the Jesus People Movement (JPM).[43] Miller found certain aspects of the diverse Jesus People Movement formed a pattern. These triggers established what he saw as the boundaries of the JPM or its distinctive. There are also distinctive elements that describe the CFM ministries. Wayman Mitchell saw certain events and occasions that led to transformation of the Prescott church. These changes produced a culture of discipleship and church planting. He said in a 2015 interview with the author, "There was a hunger and so young people began to visit our church."

A scenario emerged from the interview with Wayman Mitchell in 2015, the 2013 interview for the documentary video "Still at It," the 2013 teaching series "A Distinct People" by Wayman Mitchell and the 2015 ministry forum in Israel. The following scenario documenting the formation of the CFM is taken from these sources.

After taking the pastorate in Prescott, Mitchell attended a revival meeting in Cottonwood, Arizona. After the service he talked to the evangelist about how frustrated he was because there were no visitors at the revival. Mitchell said to the evangelist, "We have to get the gospel outside the four walls." The evangelist told him about events in California that were attracting young people to gospel events outside of churches. In late July

Mitchell took two young men and traveled to California. They took in everything they could. They visited the beach and saw an evangelist preaching and baptizing there. They read Don Pederson's *Hollywood Free Paper* and went to a service at Calvary Chapel. They visited a meeting with hundreds of young people in a La Habra community center. The Minister there had a small storefront building and a music scene and they went to it. As they sat and watched some non-professional musicians play to a crowd of probably fifty young people sitting on the floor and another fifty or so standing outside Mitchell leaned over to the two young men with him and said, "This would work in Prescott."

In late summer Mitchell brought an evangelist to Prescott for an anti-drug meeting. It was really a "crummy little program." But young people showed a lot of interest. They reached at that time some key young hippies who began to witness to their friends and family. The minister of the La Habra music scene came to minister in the Prescott church. They put on a concert in the Prescott Armory building and about two hundred young people came. The evangelist they had seen preaching on the beach came to Prescott and did a street meeting and Jesus March around the Prescott courthouse. This was all new to Mitchell.

A decision was made to rent a building and do a weekly concert called "The Door." In the fall of 1970 young people began to get saved and become part of the church. One of the hippies that got saved was about 19 and had a music group. Mitchell got them to play on the courthouse plaza and preach the gospel. "It wasn't a very good group and one of them wasn't even saved," Mitchell said. Young people responded to the music. Churches at that time rejected many of the young people with their torn Levis©, big beards and uncut hair. They were just off the streets and "We accepted them." Prescott was a redneck cowboy town. "We accepted them was the real key." This all happened in the space of a few months.

Mitchell's initial interaction with the JPM caused him to conclude several factors that began to shape the Prescott ministry. He says, "I have to admit that I did see some dynamics that worked and kind of gave us some direction. But this was not just one big plan. It was a decision here, a decision there, and the thing began to evolve." He said, "It wasn't anything that I had, or plan or scheme that I had. It was just what God was doing and we more or less followed along with what was happening." He saw that music was the trend for young people and he decided to use it. They rented and used crummy equipment, non-professional musicians and ministered outside of the walls of the church. Young people responded. Hippies responded. The church began to grow and the culture of the church changed. "And so this wasn't any plan. This was all spontaneous." But Mitchell did take note of things that seemed to work.

Mitchell saw that young people responded to young people. He began using young men to minister in the concerts. The concerts evolved into weekly Friday and Saturday night events. The young men would minister for a few minutes after music, drama, and testimonies, then do an altar call. They invited people to accept Jesus Christ as their Lord and Savior, turn from their sin and live for God. They would do two altar calls each night. Seven to fifteen salvations would be recorded each concert. The bands would also minister in other churches. Some were independent churches and some were denominational churches. In church venues outside of the Prescott church the impact was dissipated or lost. It became obvious that the fruit of these was not being retained. So a decision was made to try and retain the fruit of their labors by starting their own churches.

A brief attempt to establish a church was made in the small mining town of Kearny, Arizona. A group of people had a Bible study there and asked for a Pastor. Mitchell asked the leader of the group specifically if they meant a pastor and not simply someone to teach Bible studies on occasion. They said they wanted a pastor. So one of the early converts within the Prescott ministry was sent to Kearney. When it became obvious that he was there to build a church and preach the gospel publicly they withdrew their invitation.

Mitchell was appointed Superintendent of the Arizona Division of the International Church of the Foursquare Gospel organization. Arizona was the backside of the desert to many denominational minds. The organization had a number of run down and mostly empty buildings that nobody wanted to pastor. One of them was in Wickenburg, Arizona. This small town located about sixty miles northwest of Phoenix was a ranching community. It had a number of dude ranches that attracted tourists but the town was primarily farm and ranch people. Mitchell sent one of his early converts to a run down and empty

Foursquare building there. He sent another convert to Flagstaff and a similar mostly empty building. A third convert, the one who made the aborted attempt in Kearney, was sent to a run-down building in Tucson. There was a mother and her two children in that church. They were the congregation. It looked more like a mission than a church.

Wickenburg was immediately successful. Mitchell was astounded that a young rock-and-roll musician in an old cowboy town was a "fantastic success." Similarly, Flagstaff was a success. By the time it came to launch their third church to Tucson Mitchell says, "We knew this was working." The church was excited, "And so I didn't have to sell them, they were into that. By that time excitement had built." Church planting was not a professional operation with seminary-trained ministers. Lay ministers were planted in these churches. The Prescott church provided them with a PA and generally a guitar, guitar amp and maybe a drum kit. These early workers then moved away from family and friends to their new locations. They would have to evangelize and build relationships on their own.

Mitchell summarized what he saw as the key ingredients of these early ministries. At the very beginning Mitchell's aim was to get the gospel outside the four walls of the church and onto the streets. "What we are is evangelism and discipleship, but the real key is we are a lay movement. That means that our movement, the main stream of our movement, is not seminary trained ministers." He knows of only three persons within the CFM movement that have "actual formal theological training." He is one of them. He recalls that in the early 1970s only three persons in the Prescott ministry held credentials with the Foursquare organization though they were not formally trained in the Foursquare system. "The real genius of our fellowship is a lay movement."

Mitchell defines lay ministry saying it only means persons have not been formally educated in theology. "Many people miss this because they assume lay ministry means ignorant ministry." The process in Prescott was discipleship. It was not called discipleship at the time. Church members did not call themselves disciples. They were, however, exposed to ministry. "You must involve and motivate the lay ministry without which you cannot see sinners incorporated into the ministry [the church]." To accomplish the education and training of a lay ministry the pastor must "give himself to it."

Mitchell says that most pastors will not invest the time to be involved with lay people. Rather "they pick up with people who can be of service to them." In the CFM pastors are not encouraged to have an assistant pastor until there are two hundred and fifty or more persons in the church. The reason is so the pastor will train and use lay persons in the actual ministry of the church. If one simply pays a professional to do the ministry the lay people will not flourish and will not actually minister as needed for a culture of discipleship.

The beginning of a cultural change or transformation within the Prescott church was conversions. Mitchell's own conversion was at an altar call in Phoenix First Foursquare Church. His subsequent filling by the Holy Spirit in the same church was accompanied with the evidence of speaking in tongues. These two events established his ministry philosophy of contending for conversion and baptism in the Holy Spirit. If it happened to him then it could happen to anyone.

Conversion was a trigger that Miller identified as key to the JPM. "In short, the focus of new paradigm churches is on internal transformation as opposed to change in external appearance."[44] Although music was trending among young people the reality of the JPM was not the medium it was the message. Miller says, "In other words, while culturally current worship unquestionably attracts people to new paradigm churches, it is equally important to stress that conversion experiences focus on the *message* and not simply the *form* of Christianity [italics original]."[45] Mitchell had established the importance of conversion and baptism in the Holy Spirit prior to coming to Prescott. When he saw it happening in the JPM in California he identified with it. In more than fifty interviews and conversations with the author all expressed that they were saved or born again and the majority used the word conversion to describe the experience.

Mitchell also had grasped two other issues he saw happening in the JPM prior to coming to Prescott. One was preaching in the public arena and the other was praise. An open, public and exuberant praise was a dynamic of Jesus People worship. Another common component was preaching in coffee houses and open venues such as beaches. "We are a preaching fellowship," Mitchell says of the CFM, "and most of the world doesn't fully comprehend the importance of that." Preaching carries the image of a herald. The decree of a king was heralded. Mitchell refers to the book of Esther. The king gave a decree and the couriers took it all over the kingdom. "That's what a preacher is. He is a herald of the king." And so, "besides this being a lay movement with exuberant worship, we're a preaching fellowship."

When Mitchell was pastoring in Eugene, Oregon, he had a revelation about praise. He felt that open and exuberant praise, including tongues and lifted hands, were important to the church service. "I brought it in but it caused a disruption within the Eugene congregation." The long-term saints in the church largely opposed praise. By the time Mitchell got to Prescott he had discovered power praise. At a recent breakfast with some current pastors he said that we "accept [praise] as this is what we do. But it wasn't done in those days." Now it is an accepted part of the service. Many do not appreciate the battle that occurred early in the fellowship over open and exuberant praise in the worship service. In the early days of Prescott, Mitchell says, "I wouldn't even open the service until I had people lift their hands and praise because I wanted to establish a dimension" of God's presence in the service.

When Mitchell began to pastor in the Foursquare denomination Wednesday night was entrenched as prayer meeting night. The pastor would come and do a few minutes dissertation on prayer and then kneel down and pray. Everyone else would listen for a few minutes and then all would go home. "This is not working," Mitchell said, after three or four years. "So, I started preaching a sermon on Wednesday night and immediately it quadrupled the attendance."

Another dynamic is that of urgency. "There is this embracing of this element that Jesus could come at any time." "I preached at the last two Prescott conferences, one of my messages was that we're looking for this [return of Jesus]." This gives tremendous importance to reaping the "Last Days" harvest. Bustraan notes this of the Jesus People.

> Irrespective of variation in eschatological perspectives, the single unifying feature in the eschatology of the JP was the imminence of the second coming advent of Jesus Christ. Nearly every person interviewed for this research admitted that they felt an expectancy that Jesus could appear at any moment and consequently they felt an urgency to evangelize everyone.[46]

Bustraan saw the merging of the baptism of the Holy Spirit, missiology and eschatology as a triadic mark of the JPM. The end time imminence was also expressed in every interview the author did for this research. Bustraan questioned whether this was just the Pentecostal theology or something else. He concluded it was a unique assemblage of components comprising the JPM.[47]

Early in the 1970s a pattern was established in the Prescott Foursquare Church that would carry through to the churches planted. It also brought change to the Prescott church. The culture of the church changed. There was an acceptance of young people, ministry outside of the four walls of the church and the use of young converts to declare the gospel. This began to establish a culture of discipleship and church planting. It was something spontaneous that connected the Prescott church with "what God was doing," according to Mitchell. It begins with getting the gospel out to the people who need it. "As long as I am alive I'll never let them be diverted from that. This is evangelism, [it] is what we are all about. That is done by preaching. Evangelism is what we are called to. To take out of the Gentiles a people for His name. That's what we are called to."

Mitchell is astonished at what has occurred over the span of his ministry. "If you knew who my wife and I were and where we came from we're astonished [at] what God has done." He adds, "We were just ignorant kids, you know, absolutely ignorant. And not very many people skills." A similar wonder is found in his disciples about themselves. They had simply tried to follow what they saw God was doing in their generation. It is what Mitchell sought to do when he saw the results of the JPM in California. It was no plan or expertise they had. It was obedience in faith. Obedience brought them favor with God in the form of fruitful ministry.

# 5

# STIRRED TO REGIONS BEYOND

*"The real genius of our fellowship is it's a lay movement."*
Wayman O. Mitchell

The growth and transformation of the Prescott church continued. As Mitchell says it began with confrontational evangelism and conversions. Empowered discipleship led to a stirring of disciples to do more for God. That led to a focus on church planting. One of the young people converted in Prescott was sent out to plant a church. As mentioned the short-lived attempt in Kearney did not go well. The first attempt was not only short-lived it was marked with tragedy. This story is important because it fills in some details about how the Prescott church functioned in the early 1970s.

The Prescott church and Pastor Mitchell began to be recognized in Arizona's Foursquare organization for its tremendous numbers of conversions. A leader of a small Bible study group and prominent business owner in Kearny asked Mitchell to send a pastor. Pastor Mitchell asked Harold Warner if he wanted to go. He said yes. He told his story in an interview for the fortieth anniversary of the opening of the Tucson Church (The Door). He was a convert in the Prescott ministry and was asked if he wanted to move and pastor in Kearny, Arizona. He and another disciple traveled to Kearny. When they realized that Kearny was having a Copper Days Parade and Celebration, they got their bullhorn and followed the parade preaching the gospel. As they passed through the small downtown Warner's eyes met those of the businessman/Bible study leader. Warner said, "Our eyes met and it's almost like I knew in that moment that this was not going to be a good match. This was not a marriage made in heaven." After three days in Kearny, Warner and his friend packed up and headed back to Prescott.

We were driving back. I don't remember every detail but I do know I was driving my old Dodge Colt and there was a portion of highway that had been freshly paved with new asphalt. It had rained previously and so some of the oil had come to the surface of the road. And it was just one of those things that we hit that patch of road, the car went into a skid and when it did it came to the embankment on the side of the highway. [We] went over the embankment, rolled a number of times. When it came to rest on its wheels and I couldn't move I knew something bad had happened. I didn't know all that had happened and so the other brother went and flagged someone down who called 911.

In a Phoenix hospital Warner received the news that everything to be done for his broken back had been done. Warner would be in a wheelchair from that point on. He spent three months in the hospital. When he got out he was an outpatient for three months traveling back and forth to Phoenix from Prescott. He wore a back brace so his spine could fuse.

During his rehabilitation he was given an interview for vocational rehabilitation and a number of tests. Warner says, "I was very upfront with them that I still felt my calling was to preach the Gospel." After a long time the test results came back. "It was not their opinion that I was fit for or actually called to the ministry which was great news for me because if they're saying this man is not really fit for the ministry, then anything good that happened had to have been God."

Warner was saved in 1970. He had gotten hepatitis from shooting heroin and was living with a bunch of dope freaks when he heard about a concert at the Prescott Armory. Some of the band members had gotten saved and there were Christians there who invited him to church on Sunday. "I had never been in a Pentecostal church." He figured that worship could be lively if God was real. "I don't remember what Pastor Mitchell preached that night, but I do know that I was at the altar giving my life to Jesus." He was saved and baptized in water the same night. Regarding his call to preach Warner could not point to a specific moment or service but rather he had "a growing inner compulsion that I had a heart and a desire to communicate the Gospel." He was a young twenty-two year old who said to God, "You can take my life and [if] you can use it in any way for your glory, Lord I'm willing." Four decades of pastoral ministry have resulted and he says the compulsion is stronger now than then.

This tragedy, according to Mitchell in the 2013 interview, "broke the heart of our people and it was just a shock." On a Wednesday evening shortly after the accident Mitchell preached and challenged the congregation to believe church planting was the will of God. He said the accident was an assault from hell and challenged the congregation to respond to the will of God. He then challenged other couples to respond and rise up and take the place of Harold and Mona Warner in the call of God. Sixteen couples responded to the altar call that night. It was a turning point and crucial moment for the Prescott church, discipleship and church planting. When Warner got out of rehab he was still in a back brace. Mitchell asked Warner to preach on a Sunday night in the Prescott church. Warner said, "He didn't necessarily at that time say anything. He gave me the opportunity to preach." Granting an opportunity to minister is a key ingredient in the discipleship process.

On December 16, 1973, Warner and Mona, his wife, arrived in Tucson to pastor the Foursquare Church. Warner relates that when he began to preach there was no "fellowship" and no "pattern" of how to do things. "We just simply had a vision and that vision is still alive today." He believed if he would simply preach the gospel people could get saved and a new church could be planted for Jesus. In the 2013 interview he said,

> So, I would like to tell you today that when I went out, having been saved for the extremely long time of three years and one month that I was extremely polished, very, very eloquent and erudite, a scholar. But the reality was I was extremely raw, very naïve. I hardly knew what I was doing.

The vision and conviction that preaching would work kept him on track in the early days. It was as Warner ministered that he learned. "We learned discipleship, we learned church planting." Comparing the experience to marriage he comments that we don't get everything perfect and then get married. "No, we learn marriage." The early days of ministry in Tucson were learning days. "I learned the ministry, I learned working with people, I learned the study of the Word of God, I learned various aspects of outreach and evangelism." The tragedy and rejection that occurred in Kearny turned to a tremendous success. Tucson is today one of the premier churches in the CFM and a model for others. As the third church planted it was a time of testing for the growing discipleship and church planting culture established in Prescott.

Warner's discipleship did not end when he went to Tucson. About the time Warner was pioneering in Tucson the Prescott church was also planting a work in Nogales, Arizona. It was not going well and the decision was made to move across the border to Nogales, Sonora, Mexico. This meant Mitchell would be making trips to oversee the first expression of international ministry out of Prescott. Warner looked forward to times when Pastor Mitchell would travel through Tucson on his way to Nogales. They would simply get together. They would share their "vision." So a man sharpens the countenance of his friend. As it is often stated in the CFM, "iron sharpens iron."

There were other times when they could be together and share things about the ministry. Trips with Mitchell were part of Warner's continuing discipleship. Warner said, "You could call them mission trips with Pastor Mitchell." One of these was over the Thanksgiving weekend into Obregon, Mexico. A crusade was held in a downtown boxing arena. A number of disciples from the newly planted churches in Globe and Sierra Vista, Arizona, including the author, the author's pastor and Pastor Warner met in Obregon. During the days and evenings of the crusade there were spontaneous and informal get-togethers where pastors could talk about the ministry and gather insight from more experienced ministers. There were other trips that would not be described as mission trips but functioned much the same. Warner relates making trips with Pastor Mitchell to California to buy suits. "You know, if you are going to be a preacher you have to have a suit. And so he [Mitchell] would drive us over to the garment district in LA so that we could buy, at a reasonable price for young men who didn't have a lot of money, suits that we thought one day I'm going to wear this as I preach the gospel."

Fellowship is an important part of discipleship. Mitchell kept contact by preaching in the newly planted churches. At times Mitchell would come to preach a prophecy or end-times revival. Harold says, "I'm more convinced than ever that we are living in the last days." Prophecy revivals were an evangelistic tool. Often the so-called "Big Three" series of end time movies would be shown. These were movies about the second coming of Jesus and the rapture of the church. The idea was that one would be "left behind" if not saved or born again. They were popular evangelistic films in many churches and especially the JPM. Important, then, to the planting of the churches was the urgency of the end times. Harold called it a "foundational truth" that Jesus is coming again. It was "imparted a lot" in his discipleship and "so, I've lived with that hope." He says it is "very, very foundational to the life of any believer in any church." It stirs the urgency for evangelism.

Another foundational truth Warner says was important in establishing the work in Tucson was the baptism of the Holy Spirit. "We're still building on that. It wasn't simply a phase and then we moved on to other things." Warner says the foundation is Jesus and him crucified but then "one must be careful how one builds on that foundation to ensure continuous revival."

The prophetic type of ministry was part of the Prescott ministry that Warner experienced as a disciple and he sought to have it in Tucson. Two evangelists in particular were important. One was gifted with a word of knowledge ministry and the other was especially gifted in leading people to baptism in the Holy Spirit. Warner saw the need to establish a supernatural dimension in the church for new converts to understand that God "is the same yesterday, and today, and forever." Warner felt that the New Testament church started with an outpouring of the Holy Spirit and that same kind of ministry was possible today. He says, "I believe that the baptism of the Holy Spirit is absolutely essential for revival."

Prayer meetings and altar calls were an integral part of the church in Tucson. Warner says he has been in churches where they say they are having a prayer meeting but people just sit around talking. "I'm thinking when are they going to pray?" He found the best way to learn to pray was to actually pray. "You learned to pray by listening to other people sometimes." Corporate prayer is seen as especially important. "Being able to do it in concert with other people, a group prayer brings a dynamic that just simply praying on your own cannot."

Warner mentioned other things in the interview. His speaking betrayed the feeling and passion of deep appreciation for what has happened in Tucson. He expressed it near the end of the interview.

Am I satisfied? No. I'm satisfied that God has used me. I'm not satisfied with all that I have become. I am aware that there's still much land to be possessed in the territory called Harold Warner. So, I have not arrived. I am very grateful. That's why an anniversary, in my mind is a memorial. We are marking a specific time in order to glorify God in order to remember what God has done but always with a view of pressing on. This [church] is not a monument. We have not arrived and my prayer is that should Jesus tarry we would continue to do what we've done all these years and God would give us the grace to see a greater fruitfulness not only in our lives, but in churches we have planted around the world.

Warner provides insight to the discipleship ministry when he says, "My appreciation for the saints of God is immense." He recognizes their contribution to all that has transpired in the Tucson church. "The people, these are people who have allowed me to grow. They've put up with me learning. They embraced a pastor who still had a long way to go." He says they embraced a vision and "made it their own." Regarding discipleship he says, "It isn't just me who's made disciples. This congregation. This body of believers. They've been involved in the discipleship process as well." The Tucson church developed a culture of discipleship.

The Tucson church is over forty years old and it is still evangelizing in Tucson, working in discipleship and planting churches. It is a church-planting center. The theme of their fortieth anniversary conference was "*Still At It.*" Warner says the thought he was trying to convey with that theme was "there are certain things that we do that are distinctive of our life and our congregations. And those are good things and there is a reason why we do what we do." He knows, "There [are] some people that know what we do, but when you really grow then you know why we do what we do. And so I wanted to convey the distinctive of those things and the fact that you cannot swerve from that." Pastor Mitchell always taught us "Truth is better caught than taught." The church is a place where people can catch the truth by seeing it for themselves.

The ability to overcome setback is one test of the truth of ministry. Another test of ministry is whether it can impact another culture. The Prescott ministry entered the international arena in Sonora, Mexico. In the late 70s it entered another international arena. Contact was made in the Netherlands with a group of young converts. Contacts in Australia led to the planting of a church in Perth, Western Australia. Contacts in the Philippines led to the sending of a pastor to Manila. Shortly after that a worker was sent into Davao on the large southern Island of Mindanao and another to Cebu the largest city of the Visayas (the central islands).

Mark Aulson was saved when the personal testimony of a friend (his future wife) brought him to Arizona. He came to Prescott and was converted. He was discipled in the Prescott church and launched into ministry. After pastoring in Cortez, Colorado and Sierra Vista, Arizona he felt stirred to the regions beyond. He came to Phoenix and preached a revival for the author. He drove up in an older model K-car. Chrysler built these cars just as the corporation was about to collapse. Asked why he had downsized his car, Aulson said he wanted to get ready for greater opportunities to minister. He was trimming down his possessions.

The author accompanied him on a mission trip to the Philippines. It did not begin well. He was robbed of four hundred dollars in a money exchange. Then hordes of ants assaulted our motel room. In the course of fighting off the ants that had invaded our stash of food, he mentioned he was preparing to pioneer in Sheffield, England when we returned home. That did not work out. In a blunt appeal from Pastor Mitchell for workers to go to the Philippines Mark was challenged. He was stirred by the number of souls in the Philippines and the response to the gospel. God spoke to him, "A soul is a soul is a soul." He responded to the challenge and was launched from the conference into the city of Davao.

Mark, his wife Michele and their kids moved to Davao. The Philippines are a chain of over seven hundred islands. There is a large island in the north where the mega-city of Manila is located. There is a large island in the south, Mindanao. In between there are many smaller islands (the Visayas) and the large city of Cebu. The island of Mindanao was at that time a hotbed of revolutionaries. There were kidnappings of Catholic priests and other persons, demands for ransom, and gruesome murders. At a fellowship crusade in General Santos City in western Mindanao someone fired off a number of rounds with an automatic weapon. One of the team members, while ducking for cover, yelled out to the one preaching at the time, "Keep preaching, you're losing the crowd!" Davao is the island's largest city.

It was famous at that time for its morgue. They received bodies that had been beheaded. And then received the heads. For the morgue it was an issue of matching them to one another.

After Mark and Michelle arrived they found a place to rent and began to establish themselves in the city. Mark started witnessing immediately. One of those he witnessed to was a painter he had hired to paint the rental they had moved into. He responded to the gospel and was saved. As soon as possible Mark took him witnessing. This is how the church in Davao started. They spent nine years there before making the church indigenous. At the most recent conference the church celebrated twenty-five years of ministry. They have established a presence of God in Davao. Annual conferences attract nearly two-thousand people to their services. They do an annual parade through the downtown streets. The church is indigenous and continuing to grow. Pastors and members from over one hundred pioneer works sent out of Davao attended the anniversary conference. One of their pioneer works is in Vietnam. Nearly a dozen Vietnamese young people paid their own way to travel to Davao from Vietnam.

Another important city was Cebu. It is in the central islands of the Philippines called the Visayas. Cebu is the largest city in the region. In the beginning of the Philippine ministry teams of pastors were sent in to preach in various churches. Four pastors from the US, Europe or Australia would fly into Manila and then do revivals or conferences in various cities. Often the team would set up in the parks or plazas and show a movie. The *Ten Commandments* was popular because the 16mm version was a number of reels long. One reel could be shown each night of the week. Following the movie the pastors on the team would preach to the gathered crowd and ask for a response to the gospel. Many were saved. Then they would pray for the sick and see dramatic results. Goiters disappeared. Deaf ears opened. Blind eyes healed. The crowds were large. Often fifteen hundred or more Filipinos would gather at these crusades.

Dave Stephenson was on one of the teams that went to Davao. Dave was saved in the small Arizona town of Payson in 1977. The church there— pioneered from Prescott—was experiencing revival. He was a foreman on a construction crew when he was converted. He began witnessing to his crew. They got saved. He then became the pastor of the church. After successfully pastoring in Payson he took over the pastorate of another church. That church sent him on the mission team that ministered in Davao. He was stirred. He was so stirred that when he returned to the States he asked Pastor Mitchell at least twice and probably three times to let him pioneer in the Philippines. At the next conference in Prescott he was launched to Cebu. Six months after being in Davao, Dave and his wife and four children were in Cebu.

They spent about eight years in Cebu. The church grew dramatically and began launching pioneer churches. His wife had two more children while in the Philippines. The church continued to grow as well as his family. Today more than forty churches have been established from the Cebu church. It is a conference center and an indigenous church pastored by one of the early converts.

At the Manila International Bible Conference of 2015 the author was able to interview Alberto Desepida, the leader of the CFM churches in the Philippines. The author's involvement in the Philippines dates back to the early 1980s. Alberto Desepida was a disciple in a pioneer church at that time. The author made nine trips to the Philippines preaching revivals and teaching doctrine in several churches. It had been many years since the author had traveled to the Islands and was astounded at the great growth in the number and size of the churches. Today there are three conference churches in the Philippines. One is in Davao City on the Island of Mindanao, one is in Cebu in the Visayas and the main conference center is in Mandaluyong, Metro-Manila. Desepida is the pastor of the Mandaluyong church and leader of the Philippine churches. The CFM began ministering in the Philippines in the 1980s. The Mandaluyong church was the first pioneer work and it began in the one of the worst slums and squatter's settlements in Metro Manila. Today Mandaluyong is a hub in Metro-Manila and the site of large shopping centers.

The Mandaluyong church is a model of international church planting in the CFM. There are now over three hundred CFM churches in the Philippines. After the initial placement of a missionary in Manila, other missionaries were placed in Iloilo City, Davao, Cebu, Tacloban and Baguio City. The Philippine churches are now all indigenous works. Today there are no CFM missionaries in the country. The Philippine churches are now planting missionaries in other countries. Workers from Abu Dhabi, Guam, Indonesia, Vietnam, Macau and India attended the conference. On the concluding night of the conference seven new works were announced.

Desepida's gratefulness to the CFM for sending missionaries to the Philippines was apparent in the author's interview. He was a businessman prior to his conversion. He had worked in Libya and then started a business in the Philippines that did not succeed. Desepida was converted in Lucena City. It was a pioneer work from Mandaluyong. After two years as a disciple in Lucena City he pioneered a church. After it was established he pioneered another. Then he became an assistant in the Mandaluyong church. He is now pastor of the church and is the overseer of all the Philippine CFM churches. His desire is for others to have what he has in God. Speaking of disciples he is involved with he said, "I want them to have what I have and to know that God will work in their lives." He was talking about imparting the life of God he has experienced. His hope is to transmit it to others. He said concerning disciples in the churches, "I have faith that God will do it for them." That is, what has happened in him is possible in others. He says that the "great things" that God has done in his life are possible for others to experience. He says that even things that "seem impossible can be accomplished."

The theme he established for the May 2015 conference was "Extending the Kingdom." In the seminars conducted in the conference the topics included Turn around Churches, Discipleship, Revival and Church Planting, and Revival and Preaching. The indigenous nature of the CFM work in the Philippines is illustrated by the financing of the conference. Two rented halls were necessary to accommodate the delegates. They were air-conditioned which is unusual for the Philippines. Just the facilities cost three million Pesos (about $65,000). The airfares for the eleven delegates from Vietnam were paid along with many other air and bus fares. Food and expense money was provided for the delegates and motel accommodations for the delegates and speakers, advertising and miscellaneous expenses were raised and paid for out of the offerings taken during the conference evening services. Outside support was unnecessary.

These examples of CFM churches and the ministry are consistent throughout the interviews the author conducted. The pattern does not mean that they adhere to a program from a headquarters or have talking points. It is not "cookie-cutter" Christianity. The interviewees were passionate about the ministry and discipleship. They were passionate about establishing local churches. They see principles have been followed that work to bring about transformation in people, empower disciples and establish churches.

Transformation is a process that occurs in a local culture. The biblical and theological data show this to be a spiritual process superintended by the working of the Holy Spirit. Transformation of individuals transforms church culture. The Twelve disciples interacted with Jesus on many personal, emotional and physical levels. A. B. Bruce ennobled the first disciples as humble persons but he did not force the issue that they were especially different from the common persons of society. The diversity of the Twelve shows discipleship is a possibility for all converts.

New converts are the fuel of church transformation. New or young converts change the nature of an established church. This is what happened in the Prescott church. New converts speak the common language of the world. They have friends and relatives that are unconverted to Christ. They have access to the lost that older saints do not because their circle of friendships is mostly Christian. New converts are often persons that have time and energy for outreaching and touching new souls for Christ. They are looking for change and are willing to learn. They are willing to be disciples.

A significant moment in the CFM occurred at the 1978 international convention of the International Church of the Foursquare Gospel. Mitchell had taken young pastors to the convention and in his allotted time for speaking he let them testify. They told of their conversion and experience in ministry. Mitchell then preached the sermon, *Ministry: Opportunity for Every Believer*. In it he laid out the principles of militant evangelism and empowered discipleship. Empowered discipleship implied a ministry powered by the Holy Spirit. It also implied that real ministry is available to all believers. Every believer can experience the power of God using him or her in ministry. Immediately following conversion they can be effective soul winners. A previous speaker and denominational leader claimed that no convert should be sent to evangelize until they had been saved and trained for at least six months. That comment had triggered Mitchell. Empowered discipleship means that the disciple is actually learning and using what has been learned in real ministry situations. These are not practice exercises.

The ministry of the CFM is not practice. It is real spiritual warfare for souls. At an outreach in front of a grocery store in Sierra Vista, Arizona one of the shoppers approached and said how wonderful it was to see Christians out there preaching. She then said that her and her group where in training to become "jewels in the Kingdom." They never were seen ministering anywhere in the city. Empowered discipleship means involvement in souls who are in crisis and need helpful ministry.

It is easy to miss the point that in the CFM transformation is viewed as an impartation. It is more than theological or leadership training. If anything it could be called followership training. Jesus imparted his life into the apostles as they followed him. He gave them power and authority (Matt. 10:1; 28:18). They followed Jesus and became like him. In the CFM this process of transformation is encouraged. The aim of the CFM is to make disciples (Matt. 28:19). The goal of believers is to be disciples of Jesus. New converts minister before they are persons with titles or positions of leadership.

Three different interviewees mentioned that in the beginning no one was called a disciple and there was no pattern of ministry. It was spontaneous. Roland Allen makes this point when he writes, "Spontaneous expansion begins with the individual effort of the individual Christian to assist his fellow, when common experience, common difficulties, common toil have first brought the two together."[1] It was people in relationship with one another and with Jesus. It was in relationship with their pastor and one another that new converts learned to live as Christians. They were transformed.

The JPM was a spontaneous movement among the youth that transformed the Christianity of their generation. Roland Allen defines spontaneous:

> This then is what I mean by spontaneous expansion. I mean the expansion which follows the unexhorted and unorganized activity of individual members of the Church explaining to others the Gospel which they have found for themselves; I mean the expansion which follows the irresistible attraction of the Christian Church for men who see its ordered life, and are drawn to it by desire to discover the secret of a life which they instinctively desire to share; I mean also the expansion of the Church by the addition of new Churches.[2]

Older and experienced leaders became involved in the JPM. They established churches. Young converts became attached to these pastors. Many desired to be like them.

It was the conviction of the JPM that the gospel was the power of God (1 Cor. 1:18) to live their new life in Christ. This caused them to press for a decision about the gospel. Allen sees it as an important part of Paul's ministry. He "expected his hearers to be moved."[3] Allen did not see Paul's evangelism as merely sowing seed. It was preaching for a decision. "Further, He always contrived to bring his hearers to a point. There was none of the indeterminate, inconclusive talking, which we are apt to describe as 'sowing the seed.'"[4] In the CFM spontaneous outreaches, movies in parks, concerts and street meetings all involved preaching the gospel for decisions. It wasn't a program but it did transform churches.

In the 1970s discipleship became a common theological word. The Jesus People used it to refer to the process of growth and maturity for new converts by following a leader. It became maligned when Jim Jones and his Peoples Temple committed mass suicide. Over nine hundred members died.[5] The mass suicide was largely viewed as the downside of discipleship because they unquestioningly followed a leader to their death. In On January 18, 1982 the Air Force Thunderbirds aerobatic team crashed following the team leader in close formation.[6] The idea of closely following a leader was called into question and cult watchers began to monitor Charismatic leaders. However, following a leader is a rule of combat and essential to victory. The Air Force still flies in close formation. Discipleship is the biblical method of spiritual formation. The disciples of the JPM and CFM understood they were in a spiritual war. New converts understood they did not know how to live the Christian life. They looked for examples and leaders. They knew following a leader was essential for personal and corporate survival in a hostile world. Discipleship is following a leader in the arena of spiritual warfare. It is not simple mimicry. It is not unquestioningly following. The Twelve had a lot of questions for Jesus. The Twelve received a lot of instruction and correction. Discipleship is a biblically sound principle of following a leader and learning how to be a Christian. It is a transfer of life from one person to another.

A benefit of interviewing people is the anecdotal detail that gives insight to the emotional life of the interviewee. Their stories are valuable for understanding complex processes that have shaped their attitudes, character and lifestyle. Being a disciple is the biblical pattern of growth and maturity. In a 2013 interview a Harold Warner disciple and now a successful pastor said, "The thing that really grabbed our imagination was this whole thing about discipleship." He noticed biblically believers were called disciples before they were called Christians. He then said, "But we also understood from the New Testament that being a disciple of Jesus also meant that we would follow a man who was a God anointed leader and become a disciple of a man." A leader would prepare others in a relationship called discipleship for their destiny in God's kingdom. Significantly, he added, "The burden of discipleship was not on the pastor, but on the disciple." The pastor, the sermons, the ministry of the church would all be of value in a disciple's life. Nonetheless, he said, "This was very much something personal between me and God." The relationship between the pastor and the disciple was not just a casual one. It involved God. It involved an attachment to one another and God.

Another interviewee was converted when the Tucson church was growing to about four hundred members. In the interview he said, "Discipleship is a spirit. It's an impartation of a spirit." He said, "Pastor Warner didn't try to become who I was and I look back and admire that." That is, discipleship was not about dressing and acting relevant to a generation he didn't belong to. Warner's pre-Christian life was that of a longhaired strung-out hippie. When the interviewee who is now a successful pastor of a conference church was converted his pastor didn't look like a longhaired strung-out hippie. The interviewee was a young Mexican who had good parents. Both his mother and father were educators. He rebelled and got involved in a wild lifestyle. He likes to tell people that before he got saved he was a disciple of "Cheech and Chong." When he looked at his pastor, what he saw was a Christian. That's what he wanted. It was through the preaching of the Word, the church and learning alongside other disciples that he eventually felt called to the ministry and became a pastor. He did not spend long hours with Pastor Warner until years later when he was on staff in the Tucson church. He followed an example set by a pastor in a growing church. He developed friendships with other disciples and they stirred each other to live productively for God. He was given opportunity to minister and that led to feeling called into the ministry as a pastor.

In the CFM discipleship is an opportunity. It is not being given a job. This former Cheech and Chong interviewee said of his own ministry:

> I don't just simply hand out assignments and teach them the protocols of ministry … I do things over and over again so they can see and understand what I am doing and why I do it … It is an impartation of what he [my pastor] is in my life. [It] is what developed me as a man of God. If he had simply given me those opportunities without seeing him do it enough, I would have missed something.

He has been in the ministry over thirty years. Of those early years he says, "I wanted to emulate, not imitate." He wanted the spirit that was in his pastor. He wanted "his passion of the Word of God, his commitment to set an example, his determination to disciple men and plant churches." Looking back on thirty years of ministry he says that how he preaches, how he interacts with people and how he pastors has a "reference point" in his pastor. He is a disciple of his pastor.

Another successful pastor and conference leader talked about how he learned to minister and said, "By example, that's all I can say." It was by following an example and not close one-on-one personal encounters. He said as you were following the pastor's example, "God was speaking to you, well, this is what you need to do if you ever want to minister one day." It was a dimension of taking personal responsibility for how one lived. He said,

> You need to help another man's ministry first, so I would take personal responsibility to pick up a piece of paper off the floor if it needed to be done. I would fix this or when no one was looking, I would sweep this, clean that and you just wanted to help while you could. And so he [my pastor] taught by example.

A third interviewee echoed the thought saying about the pastor, "He showed us what to do and released us to do it." Another interviewee said the basic form of discipleship for him was learned early through the preaching and watching his pastor minister. His desire was to impart into our lives what he had and,

"I wanted to be what he was, serve God the way he served God." Impartation is difficult to put in words because it is one life being imparted to another. It involves lifestyle, vision, passion and willingness to be disciplined.

The processes of militant evangelism and empowered discipleship lead to a focus on church planting. Planting churches is a difficult, expensive and unpredictable endeavor. Church planting in the CFM compares well to the Book of Acts and the ministry of the apostle Paul. Church planting is the release of ministry from the mother church. It is the natural result of evangelism and discipleship. The gospel requires an individual decision about Jesus. Anyone can respond to the gospel. There is another result of the gospel that is often overlooked. Roland Allen wrote, "There is one other aspect of St. Paul's preaching which is often taken for granted, but it is certainly not true—that the Gospel of St. Paul was purely individualistic."[7] Paul did not preach as an isolated minister but as an Apostle of the Church of God. He gathered converts from the world into a society of believers in Christ. Paul saw them as the body of Christ. Allen says, "The first and most striking difference between his action and ours is that he founded 'churches' whilst we found 'missions'."[8] Planting new churches was the outworking of Mitchell's discovery that God was restoring the dignity of the local church. That is the local church however small or insignificant appearing has a place in God's economy. The local church has value and worth in the eyes of God. It has an honorable position in the works of the Lord Jesus. The first CFM disciples planted in local churches met a Foursquare denominational need. It quickly became obvious that discipleship brought some disciples to a place of greater ministry. They felt a calling to pioneer.

Joe Zeable was born in New York and raised in El Paso, Texas. He had attended a Catholic church until his early teens and then got involved in alcohol and marijuana. He moved to Arizona to work. He was witnessed to and was converted after watching the film *A Thief in the Night* in the Globe CFM church. He was immediately changed and delivered. He had no desire for alcohol or marijuana. His discipleship was with what he saw as a radical pastor. It was a pastor who was not ashamed or intimidated when it came to preaching the gospel. Joe grew in Christ. He became involved in ministry. At a conference in Prescott he told God, "I'm in." That is, he was committed to the ministry he saw at the conference.

God opened a door and in 1983 he began a pioneer work in Texas. After four years he came home to his mother church for a time of refreshing and redirection. In three weeks he was asked to take the pastorate of a church in a small mining town. He said, "I learned to pastor there." The church grew. They launched three churches from that small community. He began to travel overseas and minister. In four years he was again at a conference and was asked to take over a larger and long standing church. Again his ministry was enlarged and again began to plant new churches. After five years he looked back at his life and ministry. He wanted to put it in perspective. As aresult he volunteered to go overseas as a missionary. He told Pastor Mitchell that he would go "anywhere there was a need." A door to minister in South Africa opened. He went to a major seaport in South Africa and settled in a multiethnic suburb. South Africa was a race divided nation. He opened the church on a Sunday morning with fifty persons in attendance. Sunday night the crowd doubled. It continued to grow over the next eight years.

Joe Zeable is an experienced church planter and pioneer. He said it is one of the most difficult things to do. Several factors were important to his success. First was confidence. He had confidence in the gospel. He believed that if the gospel was preached God would convert people. He also had confidence in his pastor. Second was the need of a vision. Thirdly there was investment in people that were not like him. Pioneering in a foreign nation means winning people to Jesus and to oneself. It requires building relationships. In South Africa he located in an area with a large Indian population. They were predominantly Hindu. Many became converted and when they were converted their hearts changed about racism. The suburb was about sixty-five percent Indian and thirty-five percent black African. He became concerned about diversity and began to reach out to some young black men (they were just boys really) from behind the hill. His efforts began to work. Soon he pastored a multiethnic congregation in a nation where that is a rarity. He said, "We didn't have a whole lot. We had a vision." The vision for a nation and confidence in the gospel led to a thriving multiethnic church that was self-supporting, self-governing and self-propagating.

Zeable noted a significant event occurred when talking to a man after church one Sunday. The man pointed to a white Mercedes automobile. He said that the church was doing well and that Pastor Zeable would one day be driving a car like that. Joe responded saying, "No, I will not be driving a car like that. Even if I could afford it I wouldn't be driving a car like that." The man asked him "Why?" At that moment three of the young black disciples from behind the hill walked out of the church and passed the two men. They waved and said, "Good-bye pastor. See you tonight." Joe turned to the man he was talking to and said, "That's why." Joe related how those three young persons had barely enough money to get a taxi or bus to work. They did not own a car, probably never would and they would also probably never drive a car. Owning a nice car was not a thing that was morally wrong or not affordable. It was the deeper issue of the vision Joe had for the nation of Africa. A vision that was inclusive and not exclusive. It was an issue about the passion he had for souls in that nation of South Africa. It was an issue of knowing there was accountability for his example.

Ron Banet went to South Africa about fifteen years ago. After being saved and discipled in a fellowship church he pioneered. First he pioneered in Union City, New Jersey, across the River from New York, and then in the Bronx. He felt stirred to regions beyond and was given an opportunity to go to South Africa. He went to Soweto, a township near Johannesburg. Soweto became famous during the apartheid riots and was unquestioningly poor, impoverished, riddled with diseases, and slums. Ron had been a copier repair person in the US while he pioneered. In Soweto his church started with a few people and he began to disciple them. None of them had jobs. They lived in survival mode. None had a car. They walked to church.

Ron decided there was more that could be done and he started to train his disciples in how to repair copiers. It was a slow start but his ability to repair copiers for the few businesses in Soweto gave him contacts with Canon, Xerox, Minolta and other copier suppliers. They contracted out their services. He was then able to move his trainees into servicing copiers instead of doing it himself. Soon he was being called to provide service personnel. These were lucrative jobs because they came with a salary and a vehicle for making service calls. Now disciples are being placed in other cities and are pioneering churches while working on copiers. There is now a strong middle class in the Soweto church. Ron now oversees the work in Eldorado Park (also a former slum) as a national leader for over seventy churches. Ron was able to fan extravagant hope in people that at one time had no hope. There are now cars in the parking lot. In fact, parking is a problem. The point is that transformation does not stop. It continues to touch others for transformation and eventually affects their social community.

Wade Schultz was converted in 1981 and says he learned what he knows about pastoring in the church and from his pastor. He saw integrity as the primary issue. That integrity was manifest in his pastor's care of the sheep. Fruitfulness was about getting the sheep and new converts to live for God. He noticed that the pastor took personal responsibility. He said the issue was the sermon behind the sermon. That is the man doing the sermon. The preacher cannot preach beyond what he is. The disciple has to discover these principles and make them a personal possession. They are not put into disciples by demand but by example. He said the disciple learns the subtle issues by experience. By the time an empowered disciple enters the pastoral role there has been learning by experience. The experience gained by actually working with people provides the new pastor with a wealth of wisdom only gained by experience.

Long-term ministry had taught these ministers about building a foundation of discipleship in the local church. Newbigin, Van den Toren, and Hiebert have pointed out that the local church is the place of discipleship. In the local church a new convert can learn about ministry if he or she stays and works a job with people that they can relate to. A disciple who is empowered in ministry learns people skills. A pioneer pastor is on the job and learning all the time. A disciple learns by experience how to deal with diverse human personalities and reach out to other ethnic and social groups.

Roland Allen may overstate the case or seem extreme. Nonetheless there is a principle of learning that is crucial. Talking about Paul he says:

> He never proceeded by command, but always by persuasion. He never did things for them, he always left them to do things for themselves. He set an example according to the mind of Christ, and he was persuaded that the Spirit of Christ in them would teach them to approve that example and inspire them to follow it.[9]

Allen later added that Paul had confidence in his converts. "He could trust them. He did not trust them because he believed in their natural virtue or intellectual sufficiency. If he believed in that, his faith must have been sorely shaken. But he believed in the Holy Ghost in them."[10] Allen believed Paul's confidence was that Christ would care for the things Paul committed to Him and that indeed Christ would build his church.

The expectation in the CFM is that a pioneer will build after the example established in the mother church. Allen notes two things that hinder pioneering of new churches are a) over control by the mother church or supporting organization and b) the self-will of the pastor. Self-will is the natural enemy of building a church. Self-will will not translate into disciples. It produces followers that may appear to be disciples. It may produce people who do what they are told. It does not produce people who can make decisions based on principles. It does not produce disciples who can think through problems and establish a plan to deal with them. Godly zeal is the natural ally of building a church.[11] It is impossible to see the spontaneous zeal and excitement of church planting when everything is micromanaged and controlled by others who live fearing failure of their investment. The multiplication of disciples and churches is the Book of Acts pattern (Acts 6:1, 6:7, 9:31, 16:5).

# 6

# THE INDIGENOUS CHURCH

*"It isn't just me who's made disciples. This congregation.*
*This body of believers. They've been involved in the*
*discipleship process as well."*
Harold S. Warner III

In 1967 Wayman Mitchell was pastoring in Emmett, Idaho. It was a town of about 3500 people. It was founded when the Boise area had a gold strike and the two wagon roads leading into the area converged in the small valley. The gold mines closed and the region was left to farming and agriculture. He had an evangelist come and minister. Dick Mills had a gift ministry and gave Mitchell a scripture. He pointed out that Isaiah 58:12 would be the mark of Mitchell's ministry;

> Those from among you
> Shall build the old waste places;
> You shall raise up the foundations of many generations;
> And you shall be called the Repairer of the Breach,
> The Restorer of Streets to Dwell In.

Mitchell didn't see or understand all it meant at that time. He didn't have any new doctrine. He didn't have any new program. He simply decided that he would do what the Bible said. When he came to Prescott and began seeing God's move, he began to understand that the restoration of the dignity of the local church was what God was doing. It was not something that dawned on him suddenly, but it became clear as time went on and the churches and Fellowship began to take shape. It was nothing new but rather a return to the old landmarks and boundaries of the kingdom of God.

The restoration of the dignity of the local church meant a restoration of the lifestyle and disciplines of the New Testament church. It meant a restoration of biblical discipleship. It meant a place for mining the people and resources for the call of God to world impact. It meant a return to church planting out of the local church rather than a denominational headquarters. The dignity of the local church meant that there was a place in God's plan and economy for the local congregation no matter how large or where it was located. The feeling among ministers is often similar to that of a realtor—location, location, location. The key, however, was not a large city or a wealthy benefactor. It was a ministering presence of God established by obedience to God's biblical pattern.

In 1981 the author had been in the ministry two years and was pioneering a church in Roswell, New Mexico. Pastor Mitchell was holding a revival meeting in nearby Hobbs. Six or seven pioneer pastors including the author met with him for breakfast and an informal talk at his motel. It started poorly. The waitress dumped a tray of glasses filled with ice water over him. He was soaked. He jumped up saying, "It's okay. It's okay." After going to his room and changing clothes he came back and began to answer questions about pioneering.

The question came up, "What do you look for in those you want to disciple for ministry?" He listed seven traits. He started by saying, "They need to be steadfast." The disciple cannot be erratic in mood swings or behavior. They must display faithfulness to church services, outreaches and the things of God. The disciple is an example for others. He noted that God does not change (Mal. 3:6) and the command is to strengthen the feeble dimensions of one's personal life. It is necessary to make a path level for the lame or disabled to follow (Heb. 12:12-13). The disciple must personally establish a strong and steady example for others. The context of Hebrews 12 is God's discipline (12:3-11). God disciplines those he loves. It is a necessary ingredient for a successful Christian life.

One interviewee said he laughed as a new convert at the thought of being called to preach. He felt unworthy of being a disciple. But he felt very strongly God wanted his life for preaching the gospel. "So I made some radical decisions. I stepped out of college and began to focus primarily on preparing for the ministry, preparing to preach." Those decisions were related to becoming steadfast. "I made a decision that I wouldn't go to sleep without praying; that every day I would read my Bible; that I would be involved in evangelism and I would learn to work with people." Those decisions brought him to a greater expression of ministry in the church and led to pastoral ministry. Mitchell started the conversation with steadfastness. The disciple must be steadfast.

Mitchell also talked about money, relationships and fruitfulness. A disciple needs to be able to handle money and be financially solvent. He noted that it is unwise to plant a disciple in ministry that has large debt and is undisciplined in using money. He said it would be unlikely that a pioneer pastor would be able to survive at a lower pay level if there was large debt. Financial discipline had to be learned while still in the mother church. A disciple also had to be a person who could build relationships and keep them. Persons who form relationships and then jettison them for minor reasons would never be able to build a church. Churches, Mitchell said, are built on relationships. Fruitfulness is also a necessary trait. Those who are fruitful while in the body will be fruitful when pioneering. It was stated that a person in revival (personally and in a church in revival) can be planted anywhere and be fruitful. An unfruitful person in a potentially good situation would find it difficult to be fruitful. Mitchell also noted, for those at the table, that every city is hard. Disciples that are candidates for pioneering must be fruitful as soul winners and in ministry to others.

Mitchell continued explaining the need for self-motivation, moral discipline and a desire to learn. The disciple must be self-motivated. The Prescott church in 1981 had a minimal staff. There was a secretary that took care of the books, wrote the checks and paid the bills. There were a few people who cleaned the church. There was no assistant pastor. Mitchell's method of testing a potential pioneer was to put them on staff as a concert director. It provided minimal pay and a house to live in while working for the church. Mitchell commented that the concert director would not have enough to do. He could then tell if he was self-motivated. Could the disciple see needs and respond to them? Could spare time be used wisely? Could relationships be maintained while in a new position of power? Mitchell continued down his list. Morality is a primary issue in ministry. It is a personal issue to remain morally upright in a world filled with temptation. Finally Mitchell said the disciple must be a learner. In other words, could the disciple live up to the meaning of the word disciple?

Darwin E. Smith took over as Chairman of the paper company Kimberly Clark. Its stock had fallen 36 percent behind the market when he took over. He had been a quiet lawyer within the company. He wasn't too sure the board had made the right decision in selecting him. In truth the board wasn't too sure either. Under his leadership over the next twenty years the company outperformed Monsanto, 3M, Coca Cola and GE. Jim Collins, author of *Good to Great* says that in a study of *Fortune 500* companies Kimberly Clark is one of eleven out of 1425 companies that qualified as "good to great." He identified the leaders of these eleven companies as level five leaders. Darwin Smith was one of eleven out of 1425 leaders that led a company to greatness. Collins identified these leaders as similar to Abraham Lincoln. In the *Harvard Business Review* Smith was quoted saying, "I never stopped trying to become qualified for the job." The call to discipleship is a high calling. To live up to the term disciple means a standard has been set by the Twelve.

This is certainly not the only list of character issues possible. It may not be the only one Mitchell has put together or preached. It is probably not an exhaustive list. It is a good reference point. It is one list of character traits found in maturing Christians. Erwin McManus shared his concern about having a healthy church culture for producing healthy Christians.

> A person who is growing in spiritual maturity is developing emotional health. A person who is growing in spiritual maturity is healing broken relationships and building healthy ones. A person who is growing in spiritual maturity begins to take every thought captive to the obedience of Christ and no longer allows the imaginations of the heart to run riot. A person who is growing in spiritual health begins to treat his or her body as the temple of the Lord and establish personal disciplines that result in overcoming such vices as gluttony. A person who is growing in spiritual health dreams great dreams with God.[1]

The event in Hobbs illustrates the willingness of Mitchell to share his experience and methods to disciples and pioneers in the ministry.

Making disciples is a choice to become involved in another person's life and impart some spiritual gift (Rom. 1:11). It is a hands on ministry.

Interviewees all mentioned the importance of vision. Many people today simply arrive at where they are. The author pastored in the small highway town of Deming, New Mexico. There were people living in Deming who never intended or planned to be living there. They did not arrive there as a result of any plan or vision for their life. They had just arrived there. It was not a place or life they had really dreamed about. It was not the place they always wanted to live. They had no plan, no aim and no goal.

A pioneer must be a person of vision. Horace Bushnell preached in 1858 what is perhaps one of America's most influential sermons—*Every Man's Life a Plan of God*. In it he said, "God has a definite life-plan for every human person, girding him, visibly or invisibly, for some exact thing which it will be the true significance and glory of his life to have accomplished."[2] He continues noting that many give up on God when planning their lives. To young people planning their future Bushnell says, "[A] frequent mistake to be carefully avoided is that … you also give up the hope or expectation that God will set you in any scheme of life."[3] Andrew Blackwood, was a pastor, professor, and prolific author. He was from 1930-1950 one of the leading figures in American Christianity. He writes,

> There are two sorts of ministers whose careers are tragic. The first are those who do not see clearly what it is they are to do … They walk like men in a fog. The second see with some degree of clearness the destination, but they are too careless or precipitate to build the agencies by which the goal can be attained. Both classes of men arrive nowhere, the first because they do not know where they want to go, the second because they lack the wisdom of fitting means to ends.[4]

There is a tragedy in a disciple lacking vision. Blackwood goes to the point, "A minister has been ordained to an Office; too often he ends up by running an office. He was solemnly ordained to the ministry … They have ended up in a sort of dizzy occupational oscillation."[5] Part of the CFM success was in

Mitchell's ability to secure the wanderlust of the hippie generation and JPM by establishing a church and making a place for transformation to take place in a new convert's life. Disciples who stopped wandering began to grow and mature in Christ.

Vision provides a powerful energy to any ministry. It is not a blueprint from heaven providing every detail of one's life. It does require obedience to the will of God. Abraham's obedience mattered to God. Abraham did not have a blueprint for all that was to occur in his life. He had promises (Gen. 12:1-3). Joseph's dream carried him through years of setback, obscurity, loneliness, and injustice (Gen. 37-50). He never violated a position of trust or abused a place of favor. Peter was motivated by a vision to minister cross-culturally and it opened a new horizon of ministry (Acts 10-11). Gideon overheard a dream and was emboldened to attack the enemy stronghold with a small band of soldiers (Judg. 6-7). Popular choruses in CFM churches were about vision. CFM disciples expected God to impart vision to them.

Vision is considered vitally important in the CFM. God has a will. God says, "For I know the plans I have for you, declares the Lord, plans for welfare and not for evil, to give you a future and a hope (Jer. 29:11 ESV)." Vision changes how life is approached. Vision allows one to order life around a goal. A disciple could ask to do an outreach, gather some people together, ask for a band or movie and then do an outreach. He could see it happening. He had a vision of souls being converted and his or her city being changed by the power of God. It was not a programmed or planned thing. One interviewee says, "It just came out of our vision and our burden, wanting to do something for God." He said, "I think [outreaching] just came out of our own vision." In a similar way another said, "Pastor would talk about vision, you know, you have to have a vision for what God can do, a vision of our fellowship and on and on. So, I'm trying to capture that. Yeah a vision. I want to have a vision!" He prayed for God to give him a vision and believed God did. He went on and became a pastor. Another pastor described it as a common vision of the fellowship. "Our vision to this day is [to get] the gospel outside the four walls. That's what it is made for." Vision was not something for a few special converts but was something everyone needed. They were seeking a vision for their own life, for their church, and for the nations.

Following the January 1978 Prescott conference the author and another disciple were driving back home when the subject of Russia and China came up.

Russia and China in 1978 were viewed as closed nations. In the conversation one said, "Wouldn't it be great to have churches in Russia and China." That was a simple statement but the two disciples discussed it several times in the years following. In 2014 a couple from the Globe congregation was placed in Wuxi, China. Today there are thirty-four churches in China and two of them have relationship with the Globe congregation. There are over two-dozen churches in Russia and churches in other nations that in 1978 were considered closed to church planting.

One pastor came into the CFM after being saved in another fellowship in Africa. His first experience with the CFM was attending a crusade in South London. What he saw was a vision that focused on evangelism, He said, "That's when I realized, man, I need some of this." The human soul is made for great dreams. However, it is more than just a dream. The men and women of faith all died but they had "seen" something. They did not receive "the things promised." Having seen them they greeted them from afar (Heb. 11:13 ESV). They acknowledged they were pilgrims on the earth seeking a city whose builder and maker was God. They had a vision.

The church is made to change the world. Cities, suburbs, rural communities, and reservations are rife with ministry challenges. Raymond Bakke notes that, "All kinds of sexual experimentation goes on early among urban children."[6] In El Salvador people die every day from violent crimes and thirty-two percent of the gang members come from evangelical homes.[7] "The church is the agent and community of the kingdom."[8] Transformation of the city or community on any level requires vision. For a large percentage of a city to come to Christ, for broken homes to be restored, for corruption to be overturned, for truth, grace and compassion to reign there must be a people of vision. None of these things will ever come to pass without a minister with a vision for what can be. "[It] is only by living in a city, with a theological vision for the city, that we can attempt to reach the city's people."[9]

The vision for indigenous churches is vital to CFM structure and function. Conn and Ortiz, two scholars of urban ministry, address the vital work of the church in *Urban Ministry* to understand the city and God's work in it. They commented on Paul's view of the church. They say Paul saw the church in the city "as a railway station, not an exhibition hall. By both word and deed the gospel was to spread to Jew and Gentile from those communication centers."[10] Paul's mission was the transformation of society and the world by the conversion of the Gentiles. Christian's are the benefactors of all society—doing good to all.[11] This is not about being perfect. It is not accomplished in just one attempt.[12] The pastor and author Warren Wiersbe said, "When I began my ministry back in 1950, I'm afraid I didn't have a clear vision of what Christian work was all about.[13]

Vision is imparted. It does not come through a program. To have a vision it is necessary to hunger and thirst, have a desire for God, and be committed to his will. The pioneer must have a vision for the city and that vision must be imparted to those gathered together in the new church. The vision is to transform the city with the gospel. The vision is often expressed in the CFM as "We are going to change the world and nobody will know our name."

People come to church voluntarily. Vision often comes out of a personal crisis. Often, however, people are presented with a program. It can be like entering high school. The first day of class everyone is herded into the gym, sat down on the bleachers, and read the rules. They call it orientation. Ministers are often like that. A new person comes to the church and the first thing that happens is the minister or some older saint sits them down and reads them "the rules." The orientation easily overwhelms new people. They have no idea what the church's vision is, what the various activities mean, or why the congregation does the things it does. It doesn't have to be a large church for that to happen. In too many cases new people get the perception that the minister is building financial security or seeking market share. The vision is not to have the perfect church in the perfect rural or urban American city. These visitors are not perfect people. What they need to see is a vision for people like themselves. They do not yet see a vision for God's justice and God's mercy to fill the souls of the city. They do not yet see a vision of walking humbly before God and following his calling (Mic. 6:8). The vision is to bring people to Jesus and salvation. Vision creates a compelling reason for the church's existence.

Paul wrote to the Corinthians, "[Let me] show you a more excellent way (1 Corinthians 12:31 NKJV)." Jesus said, "Your love for one another will prove to the world that you are my disciples (John 13:35 NLT)." Crises shake everything in a person's life. People face suffering and sickness, fatigue and burnout, trouble and turmoil, friction and strife, and sometimes rebellion and disobedience. In every case, except perhaps rebellion and disobedience, much of the cure is a loving relationship. Gaining new converts or members is not the whole story of church planting. Birthing is not the whole story for anything living. Living things must grow, mature and reproduce. New converts must be grafted into a loving family of believers if they are to survive. Psalm 68:6, "God sets the solitary in families." The setting of persons in the body of Christ, the family of God, is a spiritual transaction. Birthing does not assure adulthood. New converts must be planted in a caring family for growth and maturity. People must be loved.

Christianity began in a conflicted world with conflicted people. Christians and Christianity embrace a new set of values. Christians view power and the use of power differently than the world. Christians do not share the same philosophy of life with the world. They share the same world but have a different value system. Those values conflict with those of society in general.[14] Love is a massive antidote for the lonely, cynical, and jaded Millenial. Most churches start with a small group or core that is living in a new value system. They must be loved. The author ministered in Kenya for a pastor who hated being there. He saw every person as a liar or thief. He didn't see any possibility of maturing new workers in the ministry. He was soon on his way back home. Bakke says, "We cannot work in our city unless we love it—its architecture, sewer system, politics, traditions and neighborhoods."[15] Mitchell says the pioneer must love the city, the ministry, and the people in the church. Roland Allen was an advocate of establishing local self-supporting, self-propagating, and self-governing churches. He did not believe they should be governed by or merely imitate Western Christianity. He wrote about the passionate heart of the believer.

> He speaks from his heart because he is too eager to be able to refrain from speaking. His subject has gripped him. He speaks of what he knows, and knows by experience. The truth which he imparts is his own truth. He knows its force. He is speaking almost as much to relieve his own mind as to convert his hearer, and yet he is as eager to convert his hearer as to relieve his own mind; for his mind can only be relieved by sharing his new truth, and his truth is not shared until another has received it. This his hearer realizes. Inevitably he is moved by it. Before he has experienced the truth himself he has shared the speaker's experience.[16]

This is passion. Passion is a crucial ingredient in discipleship. What is true for the disciple is also true for the pioneer and experienced pastor. Seeing a small group grow and become a church requires an impartation of vision, empowered discipleship, and a passionate love for a community called out and gathered together by God.

Self-control and the ability to accept correction is a vital dimension for the developing disciple. Stewardship of resources, good relationships, and fruitfulness are all related to personal discipline. The deepest levels of character are revealed when one is corrected or disciplined. Every increase and enlargement in ministry is accompanied by an increase in personal discipline.

> Do you see someone skilled in their work?
> They will serve before kings;
> They will not serve before officials of low rank.
> (Proverbs 22:29 NIV)

Richard Taylor provides insight to discipline in his book, *The Disciplined Life: The Mark of Christian Maturity*;

> Discipline is what moderns need the most and want the least.

> Too often young people who leave home, students who quit school, husbands and wives who seek divorce, church members who neglect services, employees who walk out on their jobs are simply trying to escape discipline. The true motive may often be camouflaged by a hundred excuses but behind the flimsy front is the hard core of aversion to restraint and control.

> Many nervous and emotional disorders are the accumulated result of years of self-indulgent living … The fatal weakness is unmasked in the day of trial and adversity. A lifelong pattern of running away from difficulties, of avoiding incompatible people, of seeking the easy way, of quitting when the going gets rough finally shows up in a neurotic semi-invalidism and incapacity.[17]

Maturity is found in the person with self-control who accepts ownership of their behavior. We often think the kingdom of God should be a place where training should be maximized and discipline minimized. Discipline is often equated with rules, regulations, compulsion, and punishment. But, Taylor continues, "To the Christian, discipline means discipleship—following Jesus with one's self denied and one's cross resolutely carried."[18]

There is something more than obedience or keeping the rules in discipline. Children, soldiers, students and disciples are all to come under discipline. There is more to be gained from discipline than obedience. "The aim of child discipline, or military, or academic, or religious, is a *disciplined character* which goes beyond the minimum demands of these specific disciplines and permeates the whole life. Imposed discipline ... must lead to self-discipline."[19] The ability to make decisions and order life by subjugating self is crucial for church building.

This is especially important to pioneers. If they leave their home church the structure that supports his or her character and lifestyle will remain behind. It is possible to feel they are virtually alone in a new environment and without the cultural clues of proper behavior. "In a general sense self-discipline is the ability to regulate conduct by principle and judgment rather than impulse, desire, high pressure, or social custom. It is basically the ability to subordinate."[20] The tasks of decision making, self-motivation, and maintaining emotional stability are intimately related to personal discipline. The task of self-education and having a teachable spirit are related to personal discipline. If the disciple wishes to see their vision come to fruition personal discipline is vital.

Discipline and correction are vital to the process of discipleship. It is necessary that the disciple knows accountability is a requirement. Jesus rebuked Peter (Matt. 16:23). Jesus corrected attitudes of the disciples (Mark 10:43-45). Jesus told parables that directly expressed accountability and judgment for poor decisions. All of the interviewees expressed in some way times when they knew they were being called to account for their behavior. They understood they would have to change. One currently successful and popular pastor tells of an event as a disciple when he knew he was being watched and would be held accountable. He was given opportunity to lead a large outreach in a popular city park. There were over a thousand people gathered to hear the church bands play. He was the preacher for the altar call. As he made the appeal to sinners and asked them to respond to the gospel he looked out in the crowd and saw people coming forward. Suddenly he remembered he had not brought convert cards to record the names and details of those responding. The pastor was seven feet away and also watching the response.

Talking about it later he said, "There are no convert cards, I know I am a dead man." Other disciples also realized there were no convert cards. They quickly began to tear off pieces of paper and use backs of flyers to record the details. The disciple went home that night and told his wife, "I quit. I can't do this anymore." The next day the pastor said "Good job last night." He then turned around and left. He knew he wasn't being commended for forgetting the cards. He was being commended for other aspects of the outreach and for realizing his mistake. It is not always rebuke or correction as much as knowing there is accountability for results. Empowered discipleship is real ministry that means responsibility and accountability.

The ability to run an outreach and take care of the details was an important element in discipleship. It involves ministry and responsibility. To be able to preach to a thousand sinners in a park was a great honor and privilege. It was also something watched by the pastor and if something went wrong then correction could be expected. The stories of miscues and mistakes are as many as there are disciples. Correction and direction when things do not work properly is a needed aspect of empowered discipleship. Given opportunity to minister was nothing to be taken lightly. It was understood that the souls being ministered to at any given time might not have another opportunity to hear the gospel.

On another occasion a pair of disciples were running a movie outreach. They were going to show a movie on one of the old 16mm projectors. After they were nearly set up and it was time to start they realized there was no take-up reel. One of them found a trash can and they simply ran the film's take-up footage into the trashcan. They could put it on the original reel when they finished. The ability to make things work is an important dimension of empowered discipleship. The expectation is that the person on the scene must find a way to make it work. This becomes crucial in pioneering a church. The pioneer is the one responsible for making things work. The pioneer is the one called to that city and place. The pioneer can call the pastor for wisdom, insight, and direction in many things, but ultimately the pioneer is responsible and accountable for making it work. It is the pioneer's vision and desire that has brought the new work into being.

It is a mistake to believe that these disciples are novices with little or no training. Pioneers are converts with recognized ministry. God recognizes their ministry by giving them fruitfulness. Their pastor recognizes their ministry. More importantly it is their peers who recognize their ministry. Rarely would a disciple be called to pioneer who had no proven ministry within the congregation over the course of three or more years. In one respect it is the congregation that puts their reputation on the line by supporting the disciple in a pioneer work.

Discipline, correction and rebuke are based on relationship. This is why relational attachment is important in discipleship. A typical reaction to correction is anger. Some people simply quit when they are corrected. This is especially true if there is public exposure to correction or discipline. Without relational attachment between the disciple and the pastor, correction will not accomplish the needed transformation. In an interview with an international pastor born to immigrant parents, correction was one of the biggest obstacles to discipleship. He viewed correction as rejection. Correction meant being unfit or unworthy. It could even mean being unwanted. This came from his background of rejection by his father. Biblically, discipline comes to sons because of love (Hebrews 12:3-11). It is a false love that refuses to correct. Discipline works because of a love relationship. Roland Allen's observation is that without judgment [correction] the process of human life comes to no "vivid conclusion" and moral discipline will have "no harvest."[21] Without real accountability there can be no real change. There can be obedience outwardly but no real inward change of the person. Allen wrote about Paul's use of judgment in preaching. It is, however, applicable to discipleship. Without accountability and discipline there can be no lasting change. Discipline is based on the relationship of a disciple and pastor. It is the attachment relationship that allows real correction and discipline to work in the disciples' life.

This is not control or authoritarianism. Authority and authoritarianism do not mean the same thing. In the 2008 election year, the tour leader in Israel, an American, was worried about his church and US pastor. He asked Pastor Mitchell how he controlled his members. This man had conducted many tours and observed large numbers of pastors and their congregations. He was asking because he saw the discipline and unity in the groups Mitchell had on the tour. He had noticed it on other tours with Mitchell. The reply was, "I don't control. I influence." This is based on integrity as a leader and on the relationships he has maintained over many years.

The CFM disciple is expected to grow and mature in the things of God. Growth and maturity are recognizable by the pastor and by the congregation. There is still accountability and correction. Conferences, rallies and ministry gatherings are all important throughout the course of one's ministry. Interaction with one's peers in ministry is vital. Hearing correction from a peer, from a pastor or from the Holy Spirit are signs of growing maturity and necessary for fruitful and increasing ministry.

Becoming a pastor is not the end of the story. Just as salvation is not meant to be an isolated event but connected to growth and maturity. Pastoral ministry requires continued growth and maturity. Pastors are expected to continue their self-education. They are also involved in various other avenues of ministry aimed to help them. There are conferences, training and discipleship events and evangelistic events.

Conferences are the main thrust of vision and direction for the CFM. They are held at regional sites by churches deemed to have achieved a status as church planting and discipleship models for the Fellowship. The primary CFM Conference is held in Prescott twice a year. Included in this category are events known as Harvester Homecomings. These are hosted by church planting churches that invite their own pastors back to the mother or home church. They are more local in character and shorter in duration than conferences.

Another category of ministry events can be regarded as training or discipleship events. These events include pioneer rallies, discipleship seminars and events focused on a specific group of persons such as marriage seminars, doctrine seminars and men's and women's events. These events can be area wide or more local in character. One other kind of event in this category occurred in a spontaneous way and involved only pastors. These are brainstorming sessions with open discussion and analysis of issues affecting the ministry of pastors. Often there is corroboration on sermons. These have no particular title so the author has chosen to call them ministry forums. They are very enlightening concerning the way the fellowship views world events and issues. Another type of event, although not strictly part of this category, is the twice a year business meeting. Often relevant issues are brought up that affect ministry within the

CFM. Packets of material are given to pastors that contain material to help them pastor. A number of these materials have been collected in book form as *Helps and Guidelines*.

A third category for training and encouragement is evangelistic events. These are revivals, crusades and impact teams. Crusades are held in many places and involve large outreaches or impact teams from various churches promoting an area wide crusade. They are usually advertised as healing crusades. However the main part of the message is salvation and then the demonstration of God's power in the miracles of healing at the conclusion of the message. Pastor Mitchell encourages pastors to attend these events as a learning event. They can watch the ministry and learn how to do it themselves. These three broad categories may overlap in some cases and an evangelistic component is part of almost all of them.

Conferences are major events in the CFM. They often involve large numbers of churches and large numbers of nations. Pastors and delegates from their churches come to a central location for five days. The main conference for the CFM is held twice each year in Prescott. For the Prescott conference an invitation is extended to pastoral couples of the Fellowship and to their disciples being groomed for ministry. Couples who choose to come are given five nights motel accommodation and one hundred dollars of expense money for the week. There are no registration costs and the only obligation is to attend the conference. Evening services begin on Monday night and go through Friday night. Tuesday through Friday morning three seminars are held between nine and noon. In the week there are seventeen services and seminars. The morning sessions and each evening service are preceded by a one-hour prayer service. There are two special events during the conference. Thursday night is focused on international churches and international church planting. The service begins with a video presentation of events that have taken place in the preceding six months with particular attention to overseas ministry. At the conclusion of the Thursday night service new international works and workers are announced. An offering is taken and they begin the process of moving to the country or mission announced. Friday night is the concluding service of the conference and the final event is the announcement of new domestic works being planted out of Prescott and other CFM churches. Attendance at the Prescott conference is between twenty-five hundred and three thousand in the evening services. Conferences are open to the public and non-sponsored delegates are also welcome.

The Manila conference is typical of other conferences held throughout the United States and the world. The Prescott format is maintained. The sphere of influence is more regional and not a fellowship-wide event. In Manila, for example, delegates came from the three hundred plus CFM churches in the Philippines and overseas works planted out of the Philippines. Overseas works established out of the Philippines are in the United States, Vietnam, Abu Dubai, Macao, Indonesia, and Guam. The services are conducted in Tagalog. When there are foreign guest speakers their ministry is translated. If it is an English speaker, many of the Filipinos and Filipinas are able to understand but the ministry is translated to Tagalog.

In The Netherlands the services are translated from Dutch into German, Spanish, French, Russian, Romanian, Polish and English. Non-Dutch guest speakers are translated into Dutch as they minister. The conference uses the same format. They are week-long conferences with sponsored pastors and delegates who are from regional CFM churches. The Thursday international night and Friday night announcements of new works follow the Prescott pattern. This is true of conferences the author has attended in Argentina, South Africa, The United Kingdom, Mexico, Uganda, Kenya and Sierra Leone.

Harvester Homecomings are smaller versions of the area wide Fellowship conferences. Sponsorship is extended to pastoral couples in daughter churches. The event is shorter. Often the entire homecoming occurs over a weekend. There are special speakers and extra services or seminars at homecomings. The speakers are primarily pastors discipled within and planted by the host church.

Discipleship classes and pioneer rallies are held throughout the fellowship. These events are aimed at equipping disciples for the work of the ministry. About three hundred men from CFM churches in Arizona and Nevada attend monthly discipleships in Prescott. The speakers are members of the Board of Elders and CFM conference church leaders. These classes are done for those who express an interest in public ministry. These are typically done in similar fashion in other areas of the CFM.

Pioneer rallies are designed to encourage and equip people to become involved in public ministry. These events are also designed to encourage and edify those already in ministry. Unlike discipleship classes that are just one seminar, these rallies have several speakers in three to five different sessions in one or two days. These are larger gatherings than the discipleship classes and often include pastoral couples that are struggling in their ministry. These are open to the public and have an appeal for salvation to unbelievers.

In Arizona a once yearly men's rally is held in December. Pastors and disciples from throughout the Southwest attend this annual rally. It consists of four seminars from Friday night through Saturday morning. The guest speakers, as with rallies and discipleships, are pastors with proven church planting ministry. Attendance is about twelve hundred men. Similar rallies are held in other regional areas throughout the CFM.

Other training events are conducted throughout the fellowship. The author has participated and attended doctrine and marriage seminars held in many areas throughout the fellowship. Marriage seminars are held annually in many churches and are often citywide or area wide in more rural areas. They are two-day affairs with couples encouraged to spend a night away from their kids and family to fellowship with other couples in a marriage oriented setting.

Doctrine seminars have been held throughout the fellowship but especially in third world areas where resources are limited. The author has been involved in these in South Africa, Philippines, Argentina, China and a number of other nations. These seminars are weeklong events with preaching at night and seminars during the day.

The twice-annual business meeting is a legal gathering for the conduct of in-house business and financial affairs. Nonetheless it is a place of training. Often there are legal issues that involve the ministry and cultural issues that affect churches. These are discussed and material is provided for self-education at these meetings.

Revivals and crusades are two common evangelistic types of events. They are conducted throughout the CFM and in most churches revivals and participation in larger crusades occurs several times each year. Revivals are a series of meetings with a guest speaker over the course of a week or longer. They are decidedly for evangelism with outreaches and advertising aimed at bringing new people into the church.

Transformation for the CFM is a spiritual issue that occurs in the spiritual arena of the will of God. The spiritual arena for the CFM is the local church that has a culture of discipleship. In the ministry forum in Israel (November 2015)

Mitchell stressed a number of issues about transformation through the process of discipleship. Reflecting on Matthew 28:18-20 he said, "In this scripture we see the main factors that brought our fellowship into existence." Continuing Mitchell explains,

> Discipleship is a person-to-person impartation. The common mistake is to think discipleship is about information. Personalities are shaped eyeball to eyeball. It takes time to involves one's self with another person. To disciple in a larger church you must have a culture of discipleship. We are spiritual creatures and our spirit works in others. The admonition is in 2 Timothy 2:2, "And the things you have heard me say in the presence of many witnesses entrust to reliable people who will also be qualified to teach others." Then the scripture says in the next verse, "Join with me in suffering, like a good soldier of Christ Jesus." That's the example the early church exhibits. It is by word and deed (Rom. 15:18).

Mitchell shared an example from one of the current church board members first experience in a Prescott conference. He was astounded as he walked by the prayer room and heard the "roar of our prayer meeting." People were actually calling on God with passion. Mitchell says, "That's it. We hear about prayer all the time. Here it was demonstrated and it had an impact on his life." He had been in conferences in his former denomination. He had heard sermons and seminars on prayer but in Prescott he saw it demonstrated.

Mitchell's definition of discipleship comes from Romans 1:11-12 where Paul wrote, "I long to see you so that I may impart to you some spiritual gift to make you strong— that is, that you and I may be mutually encouraged by each other's faith." Discipleship is a sincere desire to move another soul to their destiny. To impart some spiritual gift is central to discipleship. This means that the gift of life that a disciple has from Christ is to be passed on to others. As a disciple your task is to help secure the destiny of another believer. This occurs in a culture of discipleship. The task of every believer is to be involved in strengthening other believers. In a culture of discipleship believers are mutually encouraged and strengthened by one another's life of faith.

This impartation occurs not just in word. "The most successful dimension in life," says Mitchell, "comes in apprenticeship." We learn by example.

Several other interviewees echo the refrain, "truth is better caught than taught." CFM pastors see this in the relationship of Elijah and Elisha. Elisha desired a double portion of the spirit that was in Elijah. He followed Elijah. Those fifty at the school of the prophets stood and watched from a distance (2 Kings 2:1-18). Elisha observed and then did what he saw Elijah do. The result was an accomplished ministry like his master.

Mitchell's concept of spiritual transformation begins with the understanding that Christianity is not cerebral. Rather it is supernatural. It requires a "supernatural touch" that is lived out in an experience visible to others. Discipleship requires a spiritual environment where transformation can be "observed and embraced." Jesus commission to the disciples is to teach others to "observe" the things he taught. This is not just teaching of words, but teaching with a demonstration in real life of what it means to be a follower of Jesus. To "follow Jesus" means, for Mitchell, "to come and be with Jesus and become like Jesus (Matt. 8:22, 1 Cor. 11:1, 1 Thess. 1:6)." In development of a healing ministry Mitchell encourages disciples to come and watch. Mitchell repeatedly says in many contexts "anything he does can be done by others." He says you will learn more watching a crusade than in 20 years of teaching. "To observe it is to own it." It becomes your experience.

Christianity is a religion of "spiritual power," says Mitchell. This is what Paul is saying in 1 Corinthians 4:20, "For the kingdom of God is not a matter of talk but of power." The disciple is someone involved in the ministry where they can see the work of God accomplished in real lives. Discipleship gives people reference points that others can observe and then own for their own lives.

A Chinese national raised in an Atheist tradition was in the ministry forum in Israel. The entire educational system he attended in China was designed to convince him that religious people were ignorant people and to believe that the government would, through education, fix everything. He focused his life on education. He came to the United States facing divorce and having only the façade of a happy successful life. That changed when he saw people who believed God changed lives and "lived as though they were."

A pastor and fellowship leader attending the forum added that the arena of evangelism is a distinctive of the fellowship. He used the episode of the healing and deliverance of the demoniac to point out that immediately on conversion one is qualified to be an evangelist. Jesus forbids him to leave his homeland and follow him with the disciples. Instead he is told to tell those who live in his region about all that happened to him. Discipleship begins by doing what Christians do. The work in one Philippine church started when a common laborer was converted. He was then taken to witness to people about Jesus. He was immediately in the process of discipleship. He was learning by being shown how, and then given opportunity to function. According to another pastor at the forum, "Ministry is a matter of having a converted life experience to share."

An important ingredient of the CFM ministry is a converted life, that is, a demonstration of the power of Christ to change lives. In the culture of the CFM the ministry is not just about teaching. Teaching is important. There must also be a demonstrably changed life and a ministry that demonstrates the power of the gospel.

In the 2015 interview with Pastor Mitchell he confessed that there was no real plan or program that he had put in place. He literally "stumbled" into discipleship and church planting. "It took five years before I realized what God was doing," Mitchell told the author. God was restoring the "dignity of the local church." This dignity is found in the indigenous church principle.

In biology indigenous simply means a species of organism is "native" to a particular area or habitat. In the CFM the term is used to mean "from within." Indigenous means that the needs of the church are met from within. This idea has fostered the structure of the CFM. For example the Christian Fellowship Ministries is hinged to the term fellowship. It is not a denomination based upon a legal structure. It is a fellowship based on like-mindedness. In a mid-1970s Bible study called "The Church" Mitchell explained the church as "God's force in the earth." In that study a number of CFM foundations concerning the church were laid. The local church is God's plan.

Qualified ministry for the various needs of the church must be developed within the church. This does not mean that evangelists, special speakers, and other programs or ministries are precluded from being used by a local church. It does, however, mean the ministries needed to run the church must be developed by the pioneer pastor within the church's ministry as it grows. Sunday school workers, nursery workers, musicians, and other key people must be developed within the church itself. Discipleship involves people in actual ministry. This is crucial to the maturing of workers within the church. Especially dangerous is the tendency to build on "church transplants." This is discouraged in the CFM. It is not that these are evil people, although some perhaps are. People leave churches for reasons and sometimes they are not noble ones. The point is that the body grows together and is fitly framed together. The church is a living organism and grows as a unit.

Often the raw material, of building the pioneer CFM church, does not look very polished and ready for the task of ministry. Eugene Peterson, author of *The Message* was confronted by this reality in his first church. He was excited about taking his first pastorate. He anticipated building the church, seeing crowds of sinners come to Christ and pastoring. He was "astonished" he wrote in the *Christianity Today 2017 Annual Issue*, "to find men and women in my congregation yawning." He said one of the members went to sleep every Sunday morning. He always made it through the first hymn but was asleep for the rest of the service. There was an angry teenager that sat on the back pew away from his parents who read comic books. One member of the choir passed notes and whispered to her friend who provided tips on the stock market. He found hope in one member who brought a notebook to church and wrote all that he said in shorthand as he preached. He then learned that she was planning to divorce her husband and was practicing shorthand so she could get a job and support herself. The raw material for church transformation or growth doesn't always look like what they shall be. As Mitchell has often commented, the issue is not what you are but what you can become as a Christian.

The early disciples of the Prescott ministry were like much of the JPM. They were hippies, druggies and filled with wanderlust. Conversion was the first step. It was never meant to be an isolated event but an entrance into a lifetime relationship with Jesus as part of his body. These people are the raw material for all God will do through the local church.

One of the astounding lessons of the indigenous church principle is found in the raising of money to meet the needs of the church. Mitchell's mantra about money is that God will meet the needs of the kingdom through the people of the kingdom. He is adamant that the church pays her bills and that the way to raise money is not bake sales and car washes. He says, "The pastor must preach on tithing and ask people to give [money]." A local church can raise the resources to do all that God desires through the local congregation. The author took over a pastorate in a small New Mexico town. They were behind in their bills. This limited all that they could do and created a frustration in the pastor. In the midst of frustration very clearly he felt God speak to him, "You cannot afford to do all you want to do but you can afford to do all I want to do." That became a great encouragement and marked an understanding about money and God's will. He knew that if God wanted to do something that the resources would be available.

In the summer 2015 Bible conference in Prescott the cost was five hundred and twenty nine thousand dollars. During the five nights of a conference offerings are taken from the approximately three thousand persons in attendance. The Thursday night offering is used exclusively for international church planting. In four nights four hundred ninety-seven thousand dollars was given for the conference expenses and the remainder came in within two weeks. The conference was paid for. It's important to note that there are no registration fees or other fees associated with attendance at the conference. It is paid for by freewill offerings.

All of the interviewees received their training for the ministry in the discipleship of the local church. It is in the local church where the things they learned by reading, listening to sermons, going to conferences, watching their pastor and seeing other disciples were put into practice and developed. Development of ministry within the local congregation is what Bosch and Hiebert advocate, rather than the mission station approach. This is not an advocacy of ignorance. It is an emphasis on the practice of ministry as the primary methodology. In the CFM the disciples are given real ministry. There are real sinners with eternal destinies at stake in the altar calls and sermons preached by disciples. Witnessing and evangelism are to real sinners.

The indigenous church is self-sustaining, self-governing and self-reproducing. It is the place of personnel and financial resources for the ministry. It is the place of establishing converts in the faith. It is the place of training for public ministry. This is what Mitchell said he discovered in the indigenous church. This is the dignity God gives the local church.

# 7
# EPILOGUE: WILL IT LAST?

*"Church growth strategies are the death gurgle*
*of a church that has lost its way."*
Stanley Hauerwas

The story of the Prescott Foursquare Church has been written for an audience that includes lay ministers, congregations, pastors and a concerned public. The Jesus People Movement and the CFM rest on a biblical foundation within Christianity. The author's research was aimed at discovering the triggers that moved the story forward as the ministry grew. Not every story that could be told was told. Not every detail that could be noted was noted. The primary discoveries were confrontational evangelism, empowered discipleship and focused church planting. The limitations of the project meant that certain important issues were not addressed in the detail they deserve. A few remarks are necessary about the ministry of the Holy Spirit and leadership before addressing the question asked about the movement in the early 70s. "Is it a stirring on the fringes of society or is it a movement?" It is an important question. There are over seven billion souls on the earth. Most of them are not born again and many live in nations and circumstances where they have not heard the gospel. Stirrings will not change a society. Only a sustained movement has the possibility of changing society and the world.

The ministering presence and power of the Holy Spirit is of first importance in any move of God. Although the Holy Spirit has been mentioned in the text, a ministering presence has not been given the stature it deserves. The Holy Spirit is part of every aspect of the believer's life. The third person of the Godhead is crucial in calling sinners to Christ. The salvation growth, maturity and ministry of a believer is tied to the ministering presence of the Spirit. The "ministering presence of God" as it is often stated in the CFM is the tangible and real ministry of God within the church and ministry of every believer. God is everywhere. "The eyes of the Lord are in every place, keeping watch on the evil and the good (Prov. 15:3)." He is the incomparable God. But the he is at work in a ministering way in his people and his church. That is, what is happening in the church in any particular service or meeting is not the same as what is happening at the local grocery. There is a ministering presence of God. God is at work doing spiritual business. This is what Mitchell contended for in his early ministry. The public, vocal expression of worship, including tongues, was for the express purpose of establishing a forum where God could minister. Zechariah 4:6 "Not by might nor by power, but by my Spirit," and Psalm 22:3 "You are holy, enthroned in the praises of Israel," have been important reference points in the CFM.

G. Campbell Morgan (1863—1945), pastor of Westminster Chapel in London and prolific author preached his first sermon at age 13. He wrote over 80 works in his lifetime. His paper "The Purposes of the Incarnation" was included in *The Fundamentals*, a collection of nearly one hundred essays on the beliefs of the Christian faith. In a sermon on the text of Zechariah 4, he made a telling observation about the work of God and building the kingdom of God. Commenting on the familiar "it's not by might nor by power, but by my spirit" he noted that the two words might and power are very similar in meaning. In essence they are synonyms in much of the Old Testament. But he noticed a nuanced difference when the two words were used together in the fourth chapter of Zechariah.

First the word translated "*might*" is noted in the margin of the RV as "not by an army." Morgan says it means not by the force of men or of means. This is its usual translation elsewhere in the Old Testament. The connotation of the Hebrew word is the amassing of resources. These might be men, armies and/or financial resources. It can even mean ethical resources or virtue. The second word, "*power*," means force as does "*might*." But it is not used in the same sense. "*Might*" calls for an amassing of force or forces, but "*power*" does not mean just an amassing of force. Rather it is force used in a persistent way. It is strength used purposefully or vigorously.

Morgan does not offer a translation but offers an interpretation. For the word "*might*" he offers the idea of resources. It is the gathering of resources as gathering an army or money or some other necessary resource for battle and conquest. For the word "*power*" he offers the idea of resoluteness. It means a persistent use of force to obtain an objective. So that in the final analysis no matter how wonderful or great the resources and no matter how valiant and resolute the force might be, it cannot finally accomplish the purposes of God. Morgan says:

> Briefly, comprehensively then, this is the meaning of the passage: Not by anything man can do, can man do anything for God. We are very far from believing that. If I were asked today to give what I think to be the reason for the comparative failure of the Church of God in missionary enterprise, I would say that we are terribly in danger of imagining that by our own splendid resources and resoluteness we can accomplish the work, and of forgetting the superhuman factor, without which the work of God can never be accomplished.

Of course G. Campbell Morgan was not negating that we need to amass our resources and be relentless in the call of Christ.[1] The point he was making is simply that without the presence of the Holy Spirit, our efforts are not enough.

CFM success in reaching many nations has been by the ministering presence of God. It has been by the Spirit. It is always a danger when we begin to believe that success, resources, virtue and accomplishment can bring or continue the work that only God does by his Holy Spirit. This is part of the story of Gideon and the amassing of a mighty army that God whittled down to a mere three hundred. The Holy Spirit was the key to victory. The ministering presence of God in leading Gideon and striking fear in the enemy resulted in a great victory. That victory was not without the human touch. Gideon commanded his three hundred troops to shout, "The sword of the Lord and Gideon (Judges 7:18)."

In a similar fashion another pastor of Westminster Chapel was D. Martyn Lloyd-Jones (1899-1981). The former surgeon become preacher was also a prolific writer. In his classic *Preachers and Preaching* he dealt with the how-to's of sermon preparation and preaching. The author read the book during a Prescott Conference before becoming a preacher; in fact, before even intending to be a preacher. Lloyd-Jones spent fifteen chapters on the "how" of preaching. Then in chapter sixteen he dealt with the need to be full of the Spirit. He notes that all of the preceding fifteen chapters are necessary. The preacher does need to pay attention to preparation and sermon delivery but must also understand the work is complementary to what is accomplished by God's Spirit.

He leads up to chapter sixteen with the story of a productive member of his former congregation in South Wales. He fell into sin and lost home and family. He came to London bereft of everything. He was ready to throw himself off the Westminster Bridge in London when the massive clock tower Big Ben stuck 6:30. The thought crossed his mind that Dr. Lloyd-Jones would just be starting to preach and decided he would walk over and listen for a while. He entered the church just as the Doctor said the words, "God have mercy upon the backslider." Literally spoken in prayer by Dr. Lloyd-Jones they were the first words the backslider heard. Lloyd-Jones said everything was made right with God. The backslider was not only restored but became an elder in the church.

Lloyd-Jones then asks a question, "What does it mean?" And he answers, "It means we are in the hands of God, and therefore anything can happen." He then asks a question of all preachers about what he calls "unction." The publishers of his books in England at that time were reluctant, even opposed to, the idea of the Holy Spirit as a present reality in ministry. He asks, "Do you always look for and seek this unction, this anointing before preaching?" This he says is the most insightful test a preacher can apply to their ministry. Unction for Lloyd-Jones is the Holy Spirit falling upon the preacher in a special manner. It is access of power.[2]

In a certain city on a certain day Jesus recognized the "the power of the Lord was present to heal" and he healed the paralytic (Luke 5:17 NKJV). Paul was also aware that ministry is by the Spirit and ministering presence of the Lord. In Acts 14:9 he perceives a certain man crippled in his feet has faith to be healed and shouting at him to stand up straight, the man did and was healed. These occasions illustrate the need to be full of the Spirit and actively walking in the Spirit for effective ministry.

Another issue that requires greater mention is that of leadership. During the course of writing the dissertation there were a number of times the author was asked for more information about Wayman Mitchell. He was an intriguing figure to the author's committee and peers. There is certainly much that could be said about him and about a number of other leaders within the CFM. The author has traveled with Pastor Mitchell and found him to be consistently the same. He rises early, regardless of the time zone. He prays. He works on sermons and he preaches. This is in spite of others struggling with jet lag, long overseas flights, flight delays, poor hotel rooms or accommodations and strange food. He is constantly involved with church members and disciples being groomed for ministry. The staff of the Prescott church remains remarkably small. He answers his own phone. He makes decisions. He counsels and talks to people. He remembers names, events and places. It is a hands-on ministry. He insists that what he does anyone can do it—and needs to do it.

One of the techniques used by those who interview is that of asking the same or similar questions over again within a lengthy interview. The interviewer is seeking inconsistencies or glosses on difficult or troubling issues for the interviewee. In the course of listening to Wayman Mitchell in interviews, doing interviews, casual conversation and reviewing stories and ideas from past sermons and teachings there is an incredible consistency. It has led many over the course of the years to say, "I heard that before," and "You already preached that." Mitchell says, "No, I just wrote this sermon today." He is not forgetful. He is consistent.

The number of leadership books and ideas are almost too numerous to count. Leadership as has been mentioned in this book in several places; the parable of the banyan and the banana and the stories of discipleship deal with leadership. Leadership in the CFM is aimed at producing disciples. Making disciples and leaving another generation with the gospel is important. A leader must be a person with a character compatible with ministry. Character in a leader is revealed in many ways. It is especially manifest in times of crisis and stress. Ministry is filled with crises and stresses. Roland Huntford writes the epic story of, *The Last Place on Earth*.[3] It is the account of the first men to reach the South Pole. It is an exciting story of adventure and exploration. In it, however, is a stunning insight to leadership.

On the morning of November 1, 1911 Robert Falcon Scott and his British team left Cape Evans on the Antarctic continent for the South Pole. The last "unexplored" place on earth. Already on his way, Roald Amundson and his mostly Norwegian team were two hundred miles ahead. It was a race to cross fifteen hundred miles of snow and ice, traverse mountain ranges, glaciers, crevasses and mount the ten thousand feet high plateau to reach the geographical point of 90 degrees south. On the night he left Scott wrote, "The future is in the lap of the gods." Amundson and his team reached the pole December 15 and returned to tell the story. Scott and his team reached the pole just a month later and never returned. It is probable that he and the remaining members of his team spent their last nine days in their tent running out of food and fuel, too exhausted to move forward. They were only eleven miles from their next cache of supplies. The letters and diaries recovered when months later a relief party found Scott and his men dead in their tent were the material of legend but not success.

Huntford's portrayal of these two leaders pointed to things crucial for success. These two explorers, both aiming for the same goal, could not have pursued it more differently. Their temperament and approach to leadership are a study in contrasts. One profound difference was how they prepared. Scott's team spent massive amounts of money on equipment and supplies but they never learned to use or steward them. They never learned to ski before arriving in the Antarctic and yet they were going to spend months on snow and ice to get to the pole. Amundson put himself and his men and equipment into the elements and tested both. Then he sought to improve both for the journey to the Pole.

Scott also ignored the lessons of past explorers. They lived on the story of the Navy's success at Trafalgar—largely viewed as an unplanned battle where gallantry and dash saved the day. The study of strategy had almost become anathema in favor of spit and polish and Navy pride. Amundson took seriously the lessons learned by Arctic explorers. One of the most important was learning that at subzero temperatures paraffin sublimates. That is, it moves from being a solid substance to a gas. It evaporates. It does so to such a degree that as much as half may disappear. Paraffin was important as fuel. Amundson took special care to seal the tins and to take extra quantities to assure they did not run out of fuel. Scott's journals are filled with bemoaning about the shortage of paraffin on the journey.

The crucial arena and difference, however, between Scott and Amundson was in dealing with men. Huntford notes that most men have a touch of morning peevishness. Amundson knew that peevish irritability had to be removed if there was to be real cooperation and camaraderie in camp. He devised a simple plan. He awarded prizes to the team member who was able to correctly guess the temperature in the morning. Ostensibly this was important in case they were without instruments. Knowing the temperature for the day's journey was important for dealing with the dogs and daily supplies. As a result all the men would make an early morning visit outside the camp. That gave them a chance to wake-up, eliminate their peevishness, get some exercise and be alone for a few moments. When back in camp for breakfast they were a happy group. The point Huntford was making was that Amundson had an ability to deal with men. He had a deft hand in dealing with men. He had what has been mentioned often in the CFM—people skills.

In a trying time a number of years ago the author was concerned about the spiritual health and decision making of a close friend. When Mitchell was asked about the issues and how it would work out he simply said, "It depends on his integrity." In other words, it was his decision. He would have to find the mind and will of God. Sometimes it is expressed as, "You will have to find out where God lives." Mitchell was not going to interfere or try and micromanage the situation. It was a decision the author's friend would have to make. Working with people is the issue of leadership. On occasion a pastor may think he is running a military base. He is not. Sometimes the church might seem like a business— it is not. Some have gone out to pastor after establishing a successful business only to return home after a short while. The kingdom is spiritual. Pastors are dealing with broken lives. "People skills" summarizes a basic issue of leadership.

Mitchell says the reason he is able to do what he does is that he is "engaged." Often he has noted that preaching is a life. The Hall of Fame right hand pitcher Tom Seaver was engaged in pitching "the best that I possibly can day after day, year after year." The compass of his life was pitching. He said:

> Pitching … determines what I eat, when I go to bed, what I do when I am awake. It determines how I spend my life when I am not pitching. If it means I have to come to Florida [for spring training] and can't get tanned because I might get a burn that would keep me from throwing for a few days, then I never go shirtless in the sun … If it means I have to remind myself to pet dogs with my left hand or throw logs on the fire with my left hand, then I do that, too. If in the winter it means I eat cottage cheese instead of chocolate chip cookies in order to keep my weight down, then I eat cottage cheese.[4]

Mitchell is engaged in preaching. It is the compass of his life.

Without question revival is an issue of sovereignty. Many will say that any move of God is simply the sovereignty of God made manifest. The sovereignty of God is certainly the ultimate cause of revival. There is, however, another sovereign involved. It is God's creation—man. Kneeling down to the dust of the earth God breathed into his creation and he became a living soul. At one point in Jesus ministry the Jews were enraged. They took up stones to murder him. They were aiming to do so because he made the claim to be equal with God. Jesus then challenged their thinking saying,

> Is it not written in your law, 'I said, 'You are gods [*theo*].' If he called them gods [*theous*], to whom the word of God [*theou*] came (and the Scripture cannot be broken) do you say of Him whom the Father sanctified and sent into the world, "You are blaspheming," because I said, "I am the Son of God [*theou*]? (John 10:34-36).

There is much for discussion here. Note, however the word God and the word gods are both translated from the same Greek word, *theo*. Simply put it means sovereign. God is sovereign. Therefore he has a will. Humankind is also sovereign and also has a will. More importantly, a choice is theirs. The call of Paul to the Philippians is to, "Work out your own salvation." Leaders have decisions to make and must make them in and by the will of God.

The question to be asked, after nearly fifty-years as a Fellowship, is the same one asked by Enroth, Ericson and Peter's[5] in 1972. Their book *The Jesus People: Old Time Religion in the Age of Aquarius* was the first substantial look at the Jesus people. Their question was, is it a stirring or is it a real movement? Their book was largely a negative reaction by mainline churches that were losing members at the time. They said, "Is the Jesus Movement a Great Awakening, or is it merely a 'Gentle Stir?'" They wrote,

> The Jesus Movement is an unorganized social movement in the sense that it is composed of widely scattered sub-groups that, although sharing common interests and certain basic concerns, are not united under a single leadership structure or clearly articulated set of goals and objectives.

They go on to note failures in the movement and in other Awakenings of the past. They then quote David McKenna from the 1971 *United Evangelical Action* magazine:

> At the present time, it [the JPM] is an eddy outside the mainstream of American life. If it is a genuinely spiritual awakening, it will also

change the direction or the quality of the stream. That is the long-range
test of spiritual awakenings that only time can answer (p. 14).

In other words—"Will it last?" It is an important question. The burgeoning
population of the world and the mounting issues of poverty, injustice and violence
threaten the fabric of society. There is an urgency about the salvation of billions of
souls. The Prescott story is just over forty-five years old. The author's home church in
Globe, Arizona celebrated their forty-year anniversary in 2016. Although the CFM
has generated churches through three and four generations it is still too early to
say it is a sustainable movement.

The beginning of the Prescott ministry was during a desperate time in
the United States and the life of the Prescott church. The church was broken.
It was maligned. Mitchell was discouraged over the denomination and religious
people who were content and unchanging. The new converts of young people
in the late 60s and early 70s were also desperate. They were strung out on drugs
or simply tired of wandering when they came to God and surrendered their
life to Jesus. For a desperate congregation with desperate people in a desperate
generation this story could prove helpful. Certainly it is a picture of what God
can do with a broken church.

The Prescott transformation is only one story. That does not make it
irrelevant to the greater Christian community. The obvious uniqueness of the
Jesus People Movement does not mean a similar social environment is the only
soil for transformation. The culture of the United States has changed in the last
fifty years. The CFM, however, continues to grow. It continues to expand even
though there have been radical cultural changes. It also continues to expand
into other nations and cultures. The core elements of this story seem applicable
to all broken churches. Transformation does not have to be birthed in the social
environment of the 1970s. Transformation is not dependent on the cultural
environment. The small rural congregation can experience revival. Jesus said
that from the time of John the Baptist the kingdom had suffered violence.
Then he added, the violent take it by force. That is to say, the kingdom is
available. It can be grasped and made a reality. The gospel, it is often noted, works.

In the fortieth anniversary of Globe's Harvesters Homecoming, one of
the International leaders delivered two messages focused on sustainability.
The congregation was encouraged to be involved personally in confrontational

evangelism and discipleship. They were warned to maintain a culture of discipleship and church planting. By giving energy to evangelism, empowered discipleship, and focused church planting they would remain fruitful and on the "cutting edge" of God's purposes. They were told that a commitment to these things would produce fruitfulness in their lives and the church. They were encouraged to be steadfast and not diverted to other issues or spiritual winds of doctrine. Discipleship, they were cautioned, could not be reduced to a program.

Roland Allen's *Missionary Methods: St. Paul or Ours* deals indirectly with the issue of sustainability. Allen seems to assume that St. Paul's methods of church planting and evangelism are sustainable because they are God's choices. Fifteen years after its first publication Allen wrote a preface to the 1927 revised edition. In Allen's preface to he establishes his thought that Paul's work is the pattern for kingdom expansion.

> I myself am more convinced than ever that in the careful examination of his work, above all in the understanding and appreciation of his principles, we shall find the solution of most of our present day difficulties. We are talking today of indigenous churches. St. Paul's churches were indigenous churches in the proper sense of the word; and I believe that the secret of their foundation lay in his recognition of the church as a local church … and in his profound belief and trust in the Holy Spirit indwelling his converts and the churches of which they were members, which enabled him to establish them at once with full authority.[6]

Two objections to his thesis were raised. First, there is a difference between the cultures of Paul's day and today. Second, that Paul's converts were drawn from the synagogue and were able to preserve the churches from falsehood. The nay-sayers claim that the Jews were a special class of people familiar with God and uniquely able to keep the doctrine pure. The claim based on these two objections to Allen's thesis of planting indigenous churches is that it was possible for Paul but impossible today.[7] Allen then challenges these objections and reasserts Paul's methods through the rest of the revised edition.

Allen establishes the main points of Paul's method. First, he responds to the idea that Paul had a strategy of targeting strategic cities with the gospel. It is true that Paul preached in the major cities and sought to come to Rome before going to the "Regions Beyond." Allen establishes, however, in chapters 2, 3 and 4 that cultural issues such as economically, politically or commercially strategic cities do not determine the viability of the gospel. Philip preached in "all the cities (Acts 8:40)." It is also true that Paul went and preached first in synagogues and among people conversant in the monotheism of the Jews. After that he went to the gentiles. It is also true that moral and social situations were different from today. Profound in Paul's day was a common belief in demons, a religious world dominated by mystery and superstition, and the moral implications of slavery. Disease and uncleanness were common in most of the regions where Paul preached the gospel. Religious practices were often intertwined with immorality. A receptive culture was not the key to success.

Allen's point is that cultures and target populations were not the key elements in establishing the churches. It was the activity of the Holy Spirit. It was the Holy Spirit that called and separated Paul for the work of the gospel. It was by the Holy Spirit that Paul was led to places and circumstances where he ministered (Acts 13:1-3). That is, Paul did not have a concrete plan of attack or a particular strategy for the ministry based on human analysis. The Macedonian call to carry the gospel into Europe was not Paul's original aim but a direct intervention by the Holy Spirit (Acts 16:6-10). Allen adds a dozen more illustrations to make his point. Culture, class, and economic or social conditions did not limit the gospel. The ministry of Paul to establish churches in Asia and Europe was not confined to certain types of cities or classes of people. It was accomplished by the superintending work and power of the Holy Spirit.

There have been objections to the thrust of Allen's argument. But Allen makes his case that in many situations it was the direction of the Holy Spirit that led Paul to certain provinces. His desire was always to establish sending churches to reach the many provincial towns and cities he passed through. This is important. To understand focused church planting does not mean a concrete plan but rather a focus on church planting under the leading of the Holy Spirit.

Allen continues in the following chapters to press the point of creating indigenous churches. He includes a chapter on miracles, one on self-support of the new churches without micromanagement by a foreign office, and one on the preaching of Paul. The ministry of the Holy Spirit with miracles, the raising of money for self-supporting churches and preaching the gospel form the core of what Allen views as important in the ministry of planting indigenous churches. Allen concludes with chapters on church organization, authority and discipline. These chapters are viewed as crucial to indigenous church planting. Allen sees these issues as important to sustaining the spontaneous expansion of the church. What Allen sees in Paul's ministry is, in his view, the norm for Christianity. It is sustainable if the principles are maintained.

The sustainability of the CFM largely rests on the ability to maintain its core evangelism for conversions, empowered discipleship of converts and a focus on church planting. This requires the superintending of the Holy Spirit and the direction of strong leadership. It requires leadership that has the qualities of steadfastness and a life of example. It means a leadership that has a capacity to become involved and committed to discipleship. One of the outstanding characteristics of Mitchell's leadership is his commitment to evangelism and discipleship. There is no question that his leadership has been essential. Though several rounds of doctrinal diversion have swept through the church world and challenged his vision, his example has remained steadfast. These are characteristics found in Wayman Mitchell. He has been unwavering.

The CFM generally has a worship style. These are generally practiced throughout the world. Attending a CFM church in Manila would resemble in many ways a CFM church in South Africa or the Netherlands. Certainly there would be language differences and the songs might seem unrecognizable. Nonetheless the basic format would be familiar. This book is not focused on these aspects of the CFM. The challenge for the author was to discover core principles that brought transformation to the Prescott church. The conclusion of this project is that the principles of evangelism, discipleship and church planting brought about a transformation in the Prescott congregation and a ministry that brought them out of brokenness to a place of dignity and influence throughout the world.

Conversion of sinners is especially important. Converted sinners change the church. Connecting their salvation event to discipleship in a local congregation is crucial to transformation. Discipleship is the process Jesus used to train people for ministry. Jesus empowered disciples to do the work of the ministry (Matt. 10:1-10). Two things are necessary. One, is a disciple willing to allow a pastor to speak into his life. And two, a pastor with enough courage to speak into his life. In the CFM, conversion of sinners and empowered discipleship led to church planting. It led to the multiplication of disciples and churches.

Important to the greater Christian community is that these principles work in a variety of cultures. Initially the JPM were primarily white males. However the ministry of the Prescott church attracted Hispanic families from the start. A few were illegally in the US from Mexico. The author tracked the kinds of people currently in CFM ministry. In the 2016 Prescott conference the opening prayer for the conference was from Danny Manygoats, a Native American pastor. Pastors who did the opening prayers the remaining nights were from Jamaica, the Netherlands, United Kingdom, and South Africa. There were twenty-three reports given by pastors. Nineteen of these were from the foreign field. There were reports from South Africa, Argentina, Ecuador, Vanuatu, Mexico, Solomon Islands, Bolivia and China. The main speakers of the conference included indigenous pastors from Mexico, the Netherlands, Russia and the United Kingdom. In addition there were Hispanic and Black speakers from the United States. Persons from the United Kingdom and the Navajo Choir provided special music for two of the five evening services. There is a true diversity throughout the Fellowship.

Maintaining the centering themes of the CFM is the dynamic of fellowship conferences. Every six months the primary International conference is held in Prescott. Other conferences are held during the year. Conferences provide interaction of disciples and churches with directive preaching and ministry. Business meetings are important in maintaining a cohesive core of legal, social and business matters. The interaction of disciples with leaders in the Fellowship and interaction of the elders and leadership with one another are important to maintaining the centering principles throughout the fellowship.

Sustainability, however, will be judged in the following generations of churches. Disciples who grow into ministry and establish churches must continue to provide strong leadership and example for new converts. Sustainability depends on evangelism for new converts. It depends on the release of the best and most productive disciples to the harvest field. These are centering principles. They keep the main thrust of the CFM on course and free from distractions. Roland Allen has correctly noted the centering of Paul's ministry around indigenous local churches that disciple and send out churches. It corresponds with much that is centering for the CFM—principles for successfully changing the world for Christ.

The attitude in the Western world is that religion will simply fade away. Many point to failures and excesses, the waxing and waning of past movements, and theological and philosophical reasons for the decline in religion. The *Washington Post*, however, has written to summarize a PEW Research study that says the twenty-first century will be more religious than the twentieth.[8] The sub-title of Roland Allen's book gives us the necessary insight to revival. He says, *Missionary Methods: St. Paul's or Ours?* The scriptures are our clue. Are we going to establish our own methods based on human ideas and cultural imperatives or will we use the biblical methods? People point to failures and say we need something new. Men fail. That is certainly the case from time to time. But God remains faithful.

# NOTES

## Chapter 1

1 Joseph A. Fitzmyer, *Romans: A New Translation with Introduction and Commentary*, vol. 33, The Anchor Yale Bible (New Haven, CT: Yale University Press, 1993), 638.

2 Martin Luther, *Commentary on the Espistle to the Romans*, trans. J. Theodore Mueller (Grand Rapids, MI: Kregel Publications, 1954), 166.

3 John Stott, Romans: *God's Good News for the World* (Downers Grove, IL: InterVarsity Press, 1994), 317.

4 Stanley K. Stowers, *A Rereading of Romans* (New Haven, MA: Yale University Press, 1994), 40.

5 Ben Witherington, *Paul's Letter to the Romans: A Socio-Rhetorical Commentary* (Grand Rapids, MI: William B. Eerdmans Publishing Company, 2004), 281.

6 Leon Morris, *The Epistle to the Romans* (Grand Rapids, MI: Wm. B. Eerdmans Publishing, 1988), 431.

7 Douglas J. Moo, *Romans: From Biblical Text … To Contemporary Life*, The NIV Application Commentary Series (Grand Rapids, MI: Zondervan, 2000), 393.

8 *Shorter Oxford English Dictionary on Historical Principles*, 5th ed. (Oxford: Oxford University Press, 2002), 3325.

9 Scott Sharrock, "Turn Around Churches!" (Paper presented at the Philippine National Conference, Mandaluyong, Manila, 2015); Thom S. Rainer, *Breakout Churches: Discover How to Make the Leap* (Grand Rapids, MI: Zondervan, 2005).

10 William D. Mounce, *Mounce's Complete Expository Dictionary of Old and New Testament Words* (Grand Rapids, Mich.: Zondervan, 2006), 749.

11 Mounce, 739.

12 Craig S. Keener, *The Mind of the Spirit: Paul's Approach to Transformed Thinking* (Grand Rapids, MI: Baker Academic), 149-152, 165-166.

13 Keener, 76-78.

14 Ernst Käsemann, *Commentary on Romans*, ed. and trans. Geoffrey W. Bromily (Grand Rapids, MI: William B. Eerdmans Publishing Company, 1980), 325.

15 Eckhard J. Schnabel, "The Objectives of Change, Factors of Transformation, and the Causes of Results: the Evidence of Paul's Corinthian Correspondence." *Trinity Journal* 26, (2005). 202-203.

[16] Käsemann, 330.

[17] Käsemann, 324.

[18] Thomas R. Schreiner, *Romans, Baker Exegetical Commentary on the New Testament* (Grand Rapids, MI: Baker Books., 1998), 643, 648.

[19] Moo, 396.

[20] Witherington, 280.

[21] James D. G. Dunn, *Romans 9-16*, vol. 38b, *Word Biblical Commentary* (Grand Rapids, MI: Zondervan, 1988), 713.

[22] Käsemann, 329. Witherington, 284. Dunn, 38b, 709.

[23] Käsemann, 327. Dunn 38b, 711.

[24] Dunn 38b, 710-711.

[25] Schreiner, 646.

[26] Dunn 38b, 716.

[27] Fitzmyer, 639.

[28] Käsemann, 329.

[29] Moo, 394.

[30] Witherington, 285.

[31] Käsemann, 327.

[32] Dunn, 38b, 717.

[33] Stott, 321.

[34] Dunn, 38b, 709.

[35] Witherington, 286.

[36] Witherington.

[37] Fitzmyer, 640.

[38] Käsemann, 331.

[39] Witherington, 286.

[40] Witherington.

[41] Dunn, 38b, 712.

[42] Dunn, 38b, 717.

[43] Stott, 324.

[44] Dunn, 38b, 713-714.

[45] Moo, 398.

[46] Moo, 399.

[47] Witherington, 287.

[48] Keener, 145.

[49] Käsemann, 330.

[50] Philip H. Towner, "Romans 13:1-7 and Paul's Missiological Perspective: A Call to Political Quietism or Transformation?" in *Romans and the People of God*, ed. Sven K. Soderlund and N. T. Wright (Grand Rapids, MI: William B. Eerdmans, 1999), 164.

[51] Towner, 164.

[52] Moo, 397.

[53] Käsemann, 328.

[54] Schreiner, 645.

[55] Stott, 323.

[56] C. K. Barrett, *The Epistle to the Romans*, Revised ed., Black's New Testament Commentary (Peabody, MA: Hendrickson Publishers, 1991), 214.

[57] Barrett, 215.

[58] Dunn, 38b. 708.

[59] John Nolland, *The Gospel of Matthew: A Commentary on the Greek Text* The New International Greek Testament Commentary, Edited by I Howard Marshall and Donald A. Hagner. (Grand Rapids, MI: William B. Eerdmans, 2005). 1261.

[60] F. F. Bruce, *The Book of Acts*. The New International Commentary on the New Testament. Revised ed. (Grand Rapids, MI: William B. Eerdmans, 1988), 268.

# Chapter 2

[1] David Di Sabatino, *The Jesus People Movement: An Annotated Bibliography and General Resource (Bibliographies and Indexes in Religious Studies)*. 2nd ed. (Lake Forest, CA: Jester Media, 2003), 6.

[2] R. T. France, *The Gospel of Matthew, The New International Commentary on the New Testament* (Grand Rapids, MI: William B. Eerdmans Publishing Company, 2007), 1107. Michael J. Wilkins, *The NIV Application Commentary: Matthew, The NIV Application Commentary: From Biblical Text . . . To Contemporary Life* (Grand Rapids, MI: Zondervan, 2004), 947. John Nolland, *The Gospel of Matthew: A Commentary on the Greek Text*, The New International Greek Testament Commentary (Grand Rapids, MI: William B. Eerdmans, 2005), 1262.

[3] Craig S. Keener, *The Gospel of Mathew: A Socio-Rhetorical Commentary*, New (previously as *A Commentary on the Gopsel of Matthew*) ed. (Grand Rapids, MI: William B. Eerdmans Publishing Company, 2009), 715; Grant R. Osborne, "Redaction Criticism and the Great Commission: A Case Study toward a Biblical Understanding of Inerrancy," *Journal of the Evangelical Theological Society* 19, no. 2 (1976), 76.

[4] Wilkins, 971.

[5] David J. Bosch, *Transforming Mission: Paradigm Shifts in Theology of Mission.* American Society of Missiology Series, No. 16. (Maryknoll, NY: Orbis Books, 1991), 57.

[6] Bosch, 56.

[7] Osborne, 79.

[8] Bosch, 57.

[9] Bosch.

[10] Donald A. Hagner, *Word Biblical Commentary: Matthew 14-28*, vol. 33b, *Word Biblical Commentary* (Dallas, TX: Word Books, 1993), 881.

[11] Hagner. *Gospel,* 33b, 881.

[12] France, 1109.

[13] France, 1108.

[14] Cleon L. Rogers, "The Great Commission," Bibliotheca Sacra 130, no. 519 (1973), 259, 262.

[15] Robert Coleman, "The Jesus Way to Win the World," *Evangelical Review of Theology* 29, 1 (2005), 77; Donald A. Hagner, *Word Biblical Commentary: Matthew 14-28*, vol. 33b, *Word Biblical Commentary* (Dallas, TX: Word Books, 1995).

[16] Rogers, 263.

[17] Wilkins, 951.

[18] Craig S. Keener, "Matthew's Missiology: Making Disciples of the Nations (Matthew 28:19-20)," *Asian Journal of Pentecostal Studies* 12, 1 (2009), 3.

[19] Keener. *Gospel,* 718.

[20] Rogers, 261.

[21] Grant R. Osborne, "Redaction Criticism and the Great Commission: A Case Study toward a Biblical Understanding of Inerrancy," *Journal of the Evangelical Theological Society* 19, no. 2 (1976), 83.

[22] Francis Wright Beare, "Mission of the Disciples and the Mission Charge: Matthew 10 and Parallels," *Journal of Biblical Literature* 89, no. 1 (1970), 13.

[23] Osborne, 73, 78-79.

[24] Keener, 2009 *Missiology.* 3. In Daniel B. Wallace, *Greek Grammar: Beyond the Basics* (Grand Rapids, MI: Zondervan, 1996), 645.

[25] Keener, *Missiology.* 19.

[26] Osborne, 85.

[27] Nolland, 1264.

[28] Harold M. Parker, "The Great Commission," *Interpretation* 2, no. 1 (1948), 75.

29 Keener, *Gospel*, 719.

30 Wilkins, 953.

31 Hagner, 33b. 887.

32 Millard J. Erickson, *Christian Theology* (Grand Rapids, MI: Baker Book House, 1985), 1053.

33 Douglas R. A. Hare and Daniel J. Harrington, "Make Disciples of All the Gentiles (Mt 28:19)," *The Catholic Biblical Quarterly* 37, no. 3 (1975), 359.

34 Nolland, 1265.

35 France, 1114.

36 Wilkins, 953.

37 Stuart Murray, *Church Planting: Laying Foundations* (Scottdale, PA: Herald Press, 2001).

38 Wayne Grudem, *Sytematic Theology: An Introduction to Biblical Doctrine* (Grand Rapids, MI: Zondervan Publishing House, 1994), 867-868.

39 Guy P. Duffield and Nathaniel M. Van Cleave, *The Foundations of Pentecostal Theology* (Glendale, CA: Foursquare Media, 2008), 430.

40 Duffield, 431-433.

41 Erickson, 1052.

42 William J. Abraham, "A Theology of Evangelism: The Heart of the Matter," in *The Study of Evangelism: Exploring a Missional Practice of the Church*, ed. Paul W. Chilcote and Laceye C. Warner (Grand Rapids, MI: William B. Eerdmans Publishing, 2008), 18.

43 David J. Bosch, "Transforming Mission: Paradigm Shifts in Theology of Mission." Vol. 16 *American Society of Missiology Series*. Maryknoll, NY: Orbis Books, 1991, 2010.

44 Richard Mouw, "Evangelism: Keeping It High on the List." Fuller Focus, no. Spring 2011 (2011), 4-5.

45 Abraham, 28-29.

46 Eckhard J. Schnabel, *Early Christian Mission: Jesus and the Twelve*, trans. Eckhard J. Schnabel, English translation, revision and expansion ed., vol. One, Two vols. (Downers Grove, IL: InterVarsity Press, 2004), 1:4.

47 Ferdinand Hahn in Schnabel, *Early*, 1:5.

48 Schnabel, *Early*, 1:5.

49 France, 1115.

50 Keener, *Missiology*, 14.

51 France, 1115.

52 Daniel L. Migliore, *Faith Seeking Understanding: An Introduction to Christian Theology* (Grand Rapids, MI: William B. Eerdmans Publishing, 1991), 210.

[53] Ian Wilson, *Unto the Ends of the Earth* (Barrie, Canada: Northstar Advertising, 1995), 19.

[54] Drum, 6.

[55] Donald Anderson McGavran, *Bridges of God: A Study in the Strategy of Missions*, Reprint of 1955 ed. (New York, NY: Wipf & Stock Publishers, 2005).

[56] Lesslie Newbigin, *The Open Secret: An Introduction to the Theology of Mission* (Grand Rapids, MI: William B. Eerdmans Publishing Company, 1995), 122.

[57] Newbigin, 127.

[58] Newbigin.

[59] Newbigin, 124.

[60] Roland Allen, *The Spontaneous Expansion of the Church: And the Causes Which Hinder It* (Eugene, OR: Wipf & Stock, Publishers, 1962, 1997). And Roland Allen, *Missionary Methods: St Paul's or Ours* (Grand Rapids, MI: Wm. B. Eerdmans Publishing Company, 1962).

[61] Keener, *Missiology*, 3.

[62] Graham A. Duncan, "Church Discipline: Semper Reformanda as the Basis for Transformation," *Journal of Theology for Southern Africa* March, 136 (2010), 72.

[63] Ralph P. Martin, "Salvation and Discipleship in Luke's Gospel," *Interpretation* 30, no. 4 (1976), 380.

[64] Martin.

[65] Keener, *Missiology*, 16.

[66] Keener, *Missiology*.

[67] Ladd, 181.

[68] Keener, *Gospel*, 721.

[69] Keener, *Missiology*, 9.

[70] Craig S. Keener, "Sent Like Jesus: Johannine Missiology (John 20:21-22)," *Asian Journal of Pentecostal Studies* 12, 1 (2009), 27.

[71] Keener, *Sent*, 29.

[72] Keener, *Sent*, 41.

[73] Keener, *Sent*, 45.

[74] Mark J. Keown, "Congregational Evangelism in Paul: The Paul of Acts," *Colloquium* 42, no. 2 (2010), 234.

[75] Keown, 250-251.

[76] Paul Bowers. "Fulfilling the Gospel: The Scope of the Pauline Mission." *Journal of the Evangelical Theological Society* 30, no. 2 (1987), 186.

[77] Bowers, 193.

[78] Bowers, 195.

[79] John Appleby. "Paul on Mars Hill: Our Role-Model for Evangelising People around Us Today." *Foundations Spring*, 51 (2004), 20.

[80] Bowers, 187.

[81] Keener, *Missiology*, 20.

[82] Darrell L Bock. *Acts: Baker Exegetical Library on the New Testament*, edited by Robert W. Yarbrough and Robert H. Stein. (Grand Rapids, MI: Baker Academic, 2007), 12.

[83] Bock, 6-7.

[84] Schnabel, *Early*, 46.

[85] Schnabel, *Early*, 37-38.

[86] S. Murray, 66.

[87] S. Murray, 67, 74.

[88] S. Murray, 38.

[89] S. Murray, 39.

[90] S. Murray, 52.

[91] S. Murray, 40.

[92] S. Murray, 51.

[93] Bowers, 187.

[94] Bowers, 188.

[95] Bowers, 188-189.

[96] Bowers, 188, 193.

[97] S. Murray, 80.

[98] Bowers, 197-198.

[99] S. Murray, 64.

# Chapter 3

[1] Richard Bustraan, *The Jesus People Movement: A Story of Spiritual Revolution among the Hippies* (Eugene, OR: Pickwick Publications, 2014), 173-175.

[2] David Di Sabatino, *The Jesus People Movement: An Annotated Bibliography and General Resource (Bibliographies and Indexes in Religious Studies)*, 2nd ed. (Lake Forest, CA: Jester Media, 2003), 7.

[3] Sabatino, 6.

[4] Sabatino, 6-7.

[5] Sabatino, 6.

[6] Sabatino, 6.

[7] Donald E. Miller, *Reinventing American Protestantism: Christianity in the New Millennium* (Berkeley, CA: University of California Press, 1997), 132.

[8] Miller, 130.

[9] Miller, 130.

[10] Miller, 9.

[11] Miller, 132.

[12] Miller.

[13] Miller.

[14] Bustraan, 176.

[15] Shorter Oxford English Dictionary On Historical Principles, 5th ed. (Oxford: Oxford University Press, 2002), 3325.

[16] Richard Foster, *Celebration of Discipline: The Path to Spiritual Growth.* (San Francisco, CA: HarperCollins, 1978).

[17] Jeffrey P. Greenman, "Spiritual Formation in Theological Perspective: Classic Issues, Contemporary Challenges." In *Life in the Spirit: Spiritual Formation in Theological Perspective*, edited by Jeffrey P. Greenman and George Kalantzis, 23-35 (Downers Grove, IL: InterVarsity Press, 2010), 26-27.

[18] Greenman, 24.

[19] Greenman, 27.

[20] Eugene H. Peterson, *Christ Plays in Ten Thousand Places: A Conversation in Spiritual Theology.* Electronic Edition (Grand Rapids, MI: Wm. B. Eerdmans, 2008), 335.

[21] Greenman, 31, 34.

[22] Mark Fields and Stephen Summerell, "Mission and Spiritual Formation: Reflections on the Experience of the Vineyard Movement." *Journal of Spiritual Formation and Soul Care* 6, no. 1 (2013), 51.

[23] Fields, 48.

[24] Fields, 49.

[25] Fields, 51.

[26] Fields, 51.

[27] Fields, 49-50.

[28] Fields, 47-48.

[29] Greenman, 35.

[30] David J. Bosch, *Transforming Mission: Paradigm Shifts in Theology of Mission.* American Society of Missiology Series, No. 16. (Maryknoll, NY: Orbis Books, 1991), 2010.

[31] Bosch, *Transforming*, 3-4.

32 Bosch, *Transforming*, 15.

33 Bosch, *Transforming*, 41ff.

34 Bosch, *Transforming*, 65.

35 Bosch, *Transforming*, 85.

36 Bosch, *Transforming*, 166.

37 Bosch, *Transforming*, 15.

38 Bosch, *Transforming*, 166-170.

39 Bosch, *Transforming*, 185.

40 Bosch, *Transforming*, 186.

41 Paul G. Hiebert, *Transforming Worldviews: An Anthropological Understanding of How People Change* (Grand Rapids, MI: Baker Academic, 2008), 307.

42 Hiebert, *Tannsforming*.

43 Hiebert, *Transforming*. 310.

44 Hiebert, *Transforming*.

45 Hiebert, *Transforming*. 311.

46 Benno Van den Toren, "Growing Disciples in the Rainforest: A Contextualized Confession for Pygmy Christians," *Evangelical Review of Theology* 33(4):306-315, October (2009), 307.

47 Van den Toren, 306.

48 Van den Toren, 310-311.

49 Van den Toren, 312.

50 David J. Bosch, "Transforming Mission: Paradigm Shifts in Theology of Mission," *American Society of Missiology Series*, No. 16 (Maryknoll, NY: Orbis Books, 1991, 2010), 169.

51 Rodney Lambert in a personal communication in Vanuatu, June 2013.

52 Thomas S. Kuhn, *The Structure of Scientific Revolutions*, 3rd ed. (Chicago, IL: University of Chicago Press, 1996).

53 Bosch, *Transforming*, 185.

54 Bosch, *Transforming*, 15.

55 Dallas Willard, *The Great Omission: Reclaiming Jesus Essential Teachings on Discipleship* (San Francisco: Harper Collins Publishers, 2006), 3.

56 Willard, 6.

57 Frank Viola and George Barna, *Pagan Christianity* (Carol Stream, IL: Tyndale, 2002, 2008).

[58] George Barna, *Revolution: Finding Vibrant Faith Beyond the Walls of the Sanctuary* (Carol Stream, IL: Tyndale House, 2005), 48-49.

[59] Barna, 113.

[60] Brian McLaren, *A New Kind of Christian* (New York, NY: Harper One, 2001). And, Philip Yancey, *Church: Why Bother? My Personal Pilgrimage* (Grand Rapids, MI: Zondervan, 1998).

[61] Reggie McNeal, *A Work the of Heart: Understanding How God Shapes Spiritual Leaders* (San Francisco, CA: Jossey-Bass, 2000), 87.

[62] Ray Stedman, *Body Life*, (Glendale, CA: Regal, 1972), 37.

[63] Greg Ogden, *Transforming Discipleship: Making Disciples a Few at a Time* (Downers Grove, IL: InterVarsity Press, 2003), Ogden, 31.

[64] Chris Shirley, "It Takes a Church to Make a Disciple: An Integrative Model of Discipleship for the Local Church," *Southwestern Journal of Theology* 50, no. 2 (2008), 208.

[65] Shirley, 210-211.

[66] James C. Wilhoit, *Spiritual Formation as If the Church Mattered: Growing in Christ through Community* (Grand Rapids, MI: Baker Academic, 2008), 15.

[67] Wilhoit, 35.

[68] Wilhoit, 33.

[69] Quoted in, Gerhard Kittel, ed. *Theological Dictionary of the New Testament*, vol. IV (Grand Rapids, MI: Wm. B. Eerdmans Publishing Company, 1967; reprint, 1999), 424.

[70] Kittel, 416.

[71] Kittel, 419.

[72] Konrad Lorenz, *King Solomon's Ring* (New York: Routledge, 1952).

[73] Desmond Morris, *The Naked Ape: A Zoologist's Study of the Human Animal* (New York: Delta Book, 1967).

[74] E. O. Wilson, *Sociobiology* (Cambridge, MA: Harvard University Press, 1975).

[75] Mario Mikulincer and Philip R. Shaver, *Attachment in Adulthood: Structure, Dynamics, and Change* (New York: The Guildford Press, 2010), 10.

[76] Mikulincer and Shaver.

[77] Mikulincer and Shaver.

[78] Alexander Balmain Bruce, *The Training of the Twelve*, 4 ed. (Grand Rapids: Kregel Publications, 1894; reprint, Kregel, 1980), 1.

[79] A. B. Bruce, 35.

[80] A. B. Bruce.

[81] A. B. Bruce, 38.

82 A. B. Bruce, 39.

83 John MacArthur, *Twelve Ordinary Men: How the Master Shaped His Disciples for Greatness and What He Wants to Do with You* (Nashville: W. Publishing Group, 2002).

84 William Barclay, *The Master's Men* (Nashville, TN: Abingdon Press, 1959, 1991).

85 William H. Willimon, *The Last Word: Insights About the Church and Ministry* (Nashville: Abingdon Press, 2000), 59.

86 Willimon, 61.

87 Willimon, 59.

88 W. E. Vine, *An Expository Dictionary of New Testament Words: With their Precise Meaning, Revised ed.* (Nashville, TN: Thomas Nelson Publishers, 1985), 320.

89 Willimon, 60.

90 Willimon.

91 Willimon.

92 Paul G. Hiebert, *Anthropological Reflections on Missiological Issues* (Grand Rapids, MI: Baker Academic, 1994), 173.

93 Hiebert, *Anthropological*.

94 Hiebert, *Anthropological*, 174.

95 Hiebert, *Anthropological*.

96 Neil T. Anderson, *Discipleship Counseling* (Ventura, CA: Regal Books, 2003), 328.

97 Anderson, 325.

98 Paul D. Stanley, and J. Robert Clinton. *Connecting: The Mentoring Relationships You Need to Succeed in Life* (Colorado Springs, CO: NavPress, 1992), 11-13.

99 Richard Nixon, *Leaders.* (New York: Warner Books, 1982), 37.

100 Nixon, 82.

101 Nixon, 127-128.

102 Nixon, 127.

## Chapter 4

1 Richard Yates Hibbert, "The Place of Church Planting in Mission: Towards a Theological Framework." *Evangelical Review of Theology* 33, 4 (Oct 2009), 326.

2 Hibbert, 327.

3 Hibbert.

4 Hibbert, 321.

5 Murray, 47.

[6] Murray, 50.

[7] Hibbert, 329.

[8] Hibbert, 325.

[9] Hibbert.

[10] Carl F. H. Henry, "The Tensions between Evangelism and the Christian Demand for Social Justice." F*ides et Historia* 4, no. 2 (1972), 3.

[11] Henry, 4.

[12] Henry, 6.

[13] Henry, 8.

[14] Henry.

[15] Henry, 5.

[16] Rodney Stark, *Cities of God: The Real Story of How Christianity Became an Urban Movement and Conquered Rome.* (New York, NY: HarperCollins, 2006), 30.

[17] Gaspar F. Colon, "Incarnational Community-Based Ministry: A Leadership Model for Community Transformation." *Journal of Applied Christian Leadership* 6, 2 Fall (2012), 16. Stark, 76-77.

[18] Howard A. Snyder, *Liberating the Church: The Ecology of Church and Kingdom* (Downers Grove, IL: Inter-varsity Press), 1983.

[19] Paul W. Chilcote and Laceye C. Warner, eds. *The Study of Evangelism: Exploring a Missional Practice of the Church.* (Grand Rapids, MI: William B. Eerdmans Publishing Company, 2008), 216.

[20] Chilcote, 215.

[21] Rene Padilla, ed. *The New Face of Evangelicalism: An International Symposium on the Lausanne Covenant.* (Downers Grove, IL: InterVarsity Press, 1976), 214.

[22] Padilla, 215.

[23] Padilla, 217.

[24] Padilla, 218.

[25] Walter Brueggemann, "Evangelism and Discipleship: the God Who Calls, the God Who Sends" in Paul W. Chilcote and Laceye C. Warner, eds. *The Study of Evangelism: Exploring a Missional Practice of the Church.* Chapter 15:219-234. (Grand Rapids: MI: William B. Eerdmans Publishing Company, 2008), 227.

[26] Brueggemann, 225.

[27] Brueggemann, 227.

[28] David Bosch, "The Structure of Mission: An Exposition of Matthew 28:16-20" in Paul W. Chilcote and Laceye C. Warner, eds. *The Study of Evangelism: Exploring a Missional Practice of the Church.* Chapter 6:73-92. (Grand Rapids: MI: William B. Eerdmans Publishing Company, 2008), 75.

29 Stephen Carter, *The Culture of Disbelief.* (New York, NY: Basic Books, 1993). 32.

30 Harvey M. Conn and Manuel Ortiz, *Urban Ministry: The Kingdom, the City, and the People of God.* (Downers Grove, IL: InterVarsity Press, 2001), 381.

31 Andrew Blackwood, *The Growing Minister.* (New York, NY: Abingdon Press, 1960), 16.

32 Robert Linthicum, *Transforming Power: Biblical Strategies for Making a Difference in Your Community.* (Downers Grove, IL: IVP Books, 2003), 70.

33 Olando E. Costas, Harvey M. Conn and Manuel Ortiz, *Urban Ministry: The Kingdom, the City, and the People of God.* (Downers Grove, IL: InterVarsity Press, 2001), 369.

34 Ray Bakke, *The Urban Christian: Effective Ministry in Today's Urban World.* (Downers Grove, IL: IVP Academic, 1987), 55.

35 Bakke. *A Theology as Big as the City.* (Downers Grove, IL: IVP Academic, 1997), 92.

36 Bakke. *Theology*, 91.

37 Conn and Ortiz, 360.

38 Alan Hirsch and Debra Hirsch. *Untamed: Reactivating a Missional Form of Discipleship.* Kindle ed. (Grand Rapids, MI: Baker Books), Location 245.

39 Hirsch and Hirsch, Location: 1028.

40 Brueggemann, 230.

41 Brueggemann, 222.

42 Brueggemann, 233.

43 Donald E. Miller, *Reinventing American Protestantism: Christianity in the New Millenium* (Berkeley, CA: University of California Press, 1997), 72.

44 Miller, 67.

45 Miller, 66.

46 Bustraan, 154.

47 Bustraan, 153.

# Chapter 5

1 Allen, *Spontaneous*, 10.

2 Allen, *Spontaneous*, 7.

3 Allen, *Methods*, 74.

4 Allen, *Methods*.

5 Jennifer Rosenberg, "1900s.about.com/od/1970s/p/jonestown.htm." Revised November 18, 1978. Accessed March 16, 2016.

6 Gary Palamara, "The United States Air Force Thunderbirds Turn 50. Accessed March 15, 2016."

[7] Allen, *Methods*, 76.

[8] Allen, *Methods*, 83.

[9] Allen, *Methods*, 149.

[10] Allen, *Methods*.

[11] Allen, *Spontaneous*.

## Chapter 6

[1] Erwin Raphael McManus, *An Unstoppable Force: Daring to Become the Church God Had in Mind* (Orange, CA: Group Publishing, 2001), 109.

[2] Horace Bushnell, "Sermons for the New Life 1: Every Man's Life a Plan of God," (nd.). http://articles.Christian.com/article11970.html (accessed 11/30/2013).

[3] Bushnell.

[4] Blackwood, 164.

[5] Blackwood, 169.

[6] Raymond Bakke, *The Urban Christian: Effective Ministry in Today's Urban World* (Downers Grove, IL: Intervarsity Press, 1987), 102.

[7] Eric Swanson and Sam Williams, *To Transform a City: Whole Church, Whole Gospel, Whole City* (Grand Rapids, MI: Zondervan, 2010), 67.

[8] Conn and Ortiz, 367.

[9] Bakke, 85.

[10] Conn and Ortiz, 147.

[11] Conn and Ortiz.

[12] Swanson and Williams, 60-61.

[13] Warren Wiersbe, *On Being a Servant of God* (Grand Rapids, MI: Baker Books, 1993, 2007), 11.

[14] Padilla, 220.

[15] Bakke.

[16] Allen, *Spontaneous*, 10.

[17] Richard S. Taylor, *The Disciplined Life: The Mark of Christian Maturity* (Bloomington, MN: Bethany House Publishers, 1962), 13.

[18] Taylor, 29.

[19] Taylor.

[20] Taylor.

[21] Allen, *Methods*, 73.

# Chapter 7

1 G. Campbell Morgan. *The Preaching of G. Campbell Morgan* Vol. VI The Westminster Pulpit (Grand Rapids, MI: Baker Book House, 2006 reprint). 53.

2 D. Martyn Lloyd-Jones. *Preaching and Preachers* (Grand Rapids, MI: Zondervan, 1971). 305.

3 Roland Huntford. *The Last Place on Earth* (London: Pan Books, 1979). 1, 358-359).

4 Angela Duckworth. *Grit: the Power of Passion and Perseverance* (New York, NY: Scribner, 2016).

5 Ronald M. Enroth, Edward E. Erickson Jr., and C. Breckinridge Peters. *The Jesus People: Old Time Religion in the Age of Aquarius* (Grand Rapids, MI: William B. Eerdmans, 1972). 239.

6 Allen, *Methods. vii.*

7 Allen.

8 Timothy Keller, *Making Sense of God: An Invitations to the Skeptical.* (New York, NY: Viking, 2016), 9.

# ACKNOWLEDGEMENTS

The author wishes to acknowledge the faculty and staff of Bethel Seminary for their guidance throughout the work on the dissertation. It would not have been possible without the author's advisor Dr. Don Reed. Dr. Jeanine Perolini and Dr. Justin Irving also offered valuable insight and direction during the project. There are many persons involved in a research project of this nature and the author also wishes to acknowledge the kindness and help of Pastor Wayman Mitchell of the Prescott Potter's House Church and the Christian Fellowship Ministries. Many of the pastors and evangelists of the Christian Fellowship Ministries were willing to be interviewed and to give insight from their spiritual journey and pastoral ministry. Pastor/Evangelist Larry Beauregard made the interviews for his 2013 film *"Still at It"* available as well as formatting and cover design. Special thanks go to the staff and council of the Globe Christian Center for support during the Doctor of Ministry program. The author also wishes to express appreciation for the encouragement and help of personal friends and especially the author's wife and family.

Although many people have been involved, all errors of omission and commission are the author's.

# ADDITONAL RESOURCES

Wayman Mitchell with John W. Gooding, *Healing: Commission, Confrontation, Compelling Witness*. (Prescott, AZ: The Potter's Press, 2003).

John W. Gooding, ed., Helps and Guidelines: *A Handbook for the Pastors, Pioneers and Workers of the Christian Fellowship Churches Worldwide*. (Prescott, AZ: The Potter's Press, 2004).

Audio-Visual material (Sermons, Bible Studies, and Conference Video) and information available from: media@worldcfm.com

Made in the USA
Charleston, SC
19 December 2016